Opening up

2 Timothy

PETER WILLIAMS

DayOne

Opening up
2 Timothy

PETER WILLIAMS

'The apostle Paul wrote to Timothy to ensure that the right patterns of ministry and church life should continue when all the apostles were dead.

To ensure proper biblical ministry into the future, we all need to understand something of that pattern. This little book will serve as a clear and simple guide for all who want to learn.

Here you will find love for Christ and his people, solid commitment to the authority of Scripture, and forthright explanations of its meaning. Peter Williams does not shirk hard issues, but neither does he dwell on them. He is not naïve about the difficulties facing Christians today, but he is not pessimistic about the future either—he is too wise a Christian and too wise a pastor for either. I gladly commend it to many readers.'

Rev Gary Benfold
Pastor, Moordown Baptist Church, Bournemouth

ISBN 978-1-84625-065-1

9 781846 250651 >

British Library Cataloguing in Publication Data available

Published by Day One Publications
Ryelands Road, Leominster, HR6 8NZ
Telephone 01568 613 740   FAX 01568 611 473

email—sales@dayone.co.uk
web site—www.dayone.co.uk
North American—e-mail-sales@dayonebookstore.com
North American web site—www.dayonebookstore.com

Designed by Steve Devane and printed by Gutenberg Press, Malta

As always, I express my warm gratitude to Ruth and Brian Kerry for their efficient labours in preparing this manuscript for publication.

List of Bible abbreviations

THE OLD TESTAMENT		1 Chr.	1 Chronicles	Dan.	Daniel
		2 Chr.	2 Chronicles	Hosea	Hosea
Gen.	Genesis	Ezra	Ezra	Joel	Joel
Exod.	Exodus	Neh.	Nehemiah	Amos	Amos
Lev.	Leviticus	Esth.	Esther	Obad.	Obadiah
Num.	Numbers	Job	Job	Jonah	Jonah
Deut.	Deuteronomy	Ps.	Psalms	Micah	Micah
Josh.	Joshua	Prov.	Proverbs	Nahum	Nahum
Judg.	Judges	Eccles.	Ecclesiastes	Hab.	Habakkuk
Ruth	Ruth	S.of.S.	Song of Solomon	Zeph.	Zephaniah
1 Sam.	1 Samuel	Isa.	Isaiah	Hag.	Haggai
2 Sam.	2 Samuel	Jer.	Jeremiah	Zech.	Zechariah
1 Kings	1 Kings	Lam.	Lamentations	Mal.	Malachi
2 Kings	2 Kings	Ezek.	Ezekiel		

THE NEW TESTAMENT		Gal.	Galatians	Heb.	Hebrews
		Eph.	Ephesians	James	James
Matt.	Matthew	Phil.	Philippians	1 Peter	1 Peter
Mark	Mark	Col.	Colossians	2 Peter	2 Peter
Luke	Luke	1 Thes.	1 Thessalonians	1 John	1 John
John	John	2 Thes.	2 Thessalonians	2 John	2 John
Acts	Acts	1 Tim.	1 Timothy	3 John	3 John
Rom.	Romans	2 Tim.	2 Timothy	Jude	Jude
1 Cor.	1 Corinthians	Titus	Titus	Rev.	Revelation
2 Cor.	2 Corinthians	Philem.	Philemon		

Overview

Paul's second letter to Timothy is warm and personal in its tone, containing the advice and encouragement of the aged apostle to Timothy, the young pastor. It also gives us a deeply moving insight into the way the great apostle, shut up in his cold damp prison cell and chained like a criminal, faced the closing days of his life prior to execution. This was very different from the house arrest with which we leave him in the closing chapter of Acts, and it asks the intriguing question: Was this a second Roman imprisonment following the fourth missionary journey?

This epistle is immensely relevant for the life of today's church. It was written when Christians were suffering persecution under the Emperor Nero, and when falsehood had become fashionable within the church itself. But Paul urges Timothy not to yield to the pressures of the age, but to 'preach the Word in season and out of season', and to remain faithful to the Apostolic faith. That is a message we need to take to heart today.

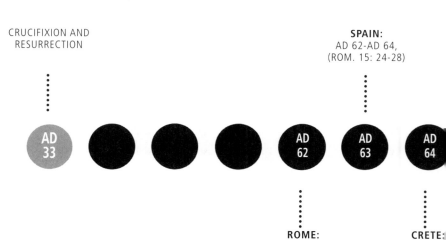

CRUCIFIXION AND
RESURRECTION

SPAIN:
AD 62-AD 64,
(ROM. 15: 24-28)

AD 33   AD 62   AD 63   AD 64

ROME:
RELEASED FROM
PRISON AD 62

CRETE:
AD 64-6
(TITUS 1:

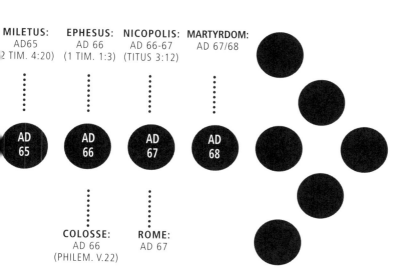

MILETUS:	EPHESUS:	NICOPOLIS:	MARTYRDOM:
AD65	AD 66	AD 66-67	AD 67/68
2 TIM. 4:20)	(1 TIM. 1:3)	(TITUS 3:12)	

AD 65 — AD 66 — AD 67 — AD 68

COLOSSE: AD 66 (PHILEM. V.22)

ROME: AD 67

Background to 2 Timothy

Paul's first and second letters to Timothy, together with that to Titus, are commonly known as the Pastoral Epistles because they are written to individuals rather than churches. But while this gives them a more 'personal' feel and includes some intimate and loving details not found in Paul's other epistles, this does not mean that they have nothing to say to the churches. They deal with various pastoral matters such as worship, false teaching, the social relief of widows and the selection of elders and deacons.

In this second letter to Timothy, Paul is chiefly concerned to remind him that, as a pastor, the 'deposit' of the gospel has been entrusted to his care and that he is to preach it faithfully and ensure that it is transmitted to other faithful men who will teach it to future generations.

This is a message that is highly relevant today when the church appears to be so confused regarding the message it is called to proclaim to our modern world.

Circumstances of writing

There is some disagreement among bible scholars as to the

actual date when Paul wrote this second letter, but we can be virtually certain that it was between AD 64 and AD 67 during his imprisonment in Rome. From the chronology in Acts we know that Paul made three missionary journeys—Acts 13 and 14, Acts 16:40-18:22, and Acts 18:23f which ended with his imprisonment in Rome, Acts 28:30.

But there are strong reasons for believing that he was released from prison in Rome and undertook a fourth missionary journey when he may have fulfilled his intention to visit Spain (Rom. 15:24). Other places he may have visited on this fourth journey are mentioned in the Pastoral Epistles and in his other letters (see map on page 9). During this journey, he left Timothy in charge of the church at Ephesus (1 Tim. 1:3-4), and continued to Rome where he was imprisoned for a second time. It was during this second imprisonment (2 Tim. 2:9) that he wrote this second letter knowing that his death was fast approaching: 'For I am already being poured out like a drink offering, and the time has come for my departure' (2 Tim. 4:6).

During this second imprisonment, the persecution of Christians under Nero was at its height, and Paul's circumstances were very different from the house arrest mentioned in Acts 28. He was now in a cold, dark dungeon 'suffering even to the point of being chained like a criminal, (2 Tim. 2:9). According to ancient tradition he was executed on the Osian Way outside Rome around AD 67.

Why study 2 Timothy?

There are several good reasons for doing so.

1. From Paul's imprisonment and his attitude in the face of

certain execution we can learn as Christians how to face the extremities of life.

2. Like Timothy, we all have our God-given gifts, but Paul's exhortation to him to 'stir up' his gift teaches us that the responsibility is ours for the use we make of our gifts.

3. The warmth of affection that existed between Paul and Timothy, and which is amply demonstrated in this epistle, teaches us the worth of fellowship among believers.

4. We learn how the 'deposit' of the gospel has been entrusted to us as it was to Timothy, and like him we are to pass it on to others.

5. It teaches us that the most effective way to combat false teaching in the church is through the preaching of sound doctrine.

6. It presents us with the solemn truth that as history draws to its close and the coming of Christ grows ever nearer, we can expect the world situation to deteriorate, and living the Christian life to become more challenging.

7. We learn that the Holy Scriptures are inspired by the Holy Spirit, and how we are to use them for the work of ministry and witness.

8. It outlines the work of the pastorate and emphasizes the preaching of the gospel as the most important element of that work.

Who was Timothy?

From the many references in Scripture we can put together a very comprehensive picture of Timothy. A good introduction is given in Acts 16 where we are told of Paul's visit to Lystra.

'He came to Derbe and then to Lystra, where a disciple

named Timothy lived, whose mother was a Jewess and a believer, but whose father was a Greek. The brothers at Lystra and Iconium spoke well of him. Paul wanted to take him along on the journey, so he circumcised him because of the Jews who lived in that area, for they all knew that his father was a Greek' (Acts 16:1-3)

Timothy was the son of a mixed marriage, and in all probability he was converted under Paul's ministry during an earlier visit to Lystra on his first missionary journey. Timothy was a godly young man and, according to the passage above, he was given a good testimony by the brethren of his hometown, which must have influenced Paul's decision to have him as a travelling companion. The apostle had a deep and affectionate regard for the young man and in his first epistle describes him as 'my true son in the faith' (1 Tim. 1:2).

From the many references in Scripture we can put together a very comprehensive picture of Timothy. A good introduction is given in Acts 16 where we are told of Paul's visit to Lystra.

As an unbeliever, Timothy's father would have had no part in his spiritual upbringing, but both his mother, Eunice, and his grandmother, Lois, were Christians and had a determining influence upon him (2 Tim. 1:5). There is no doubt he was a highly gifted young man and received a special endowment of the Holy Spirit for the leadership role he was to have in the early church. Paul refers to 'the prophecies once made about you' (1 Tim. 1:18), and urges him not to 'neglect your gift, which was given you through a prophetic message when the body of elders laid their hands on you' (1 Tim. 4:14).

When it comes to character and temperament, Timothy seems to have had a very low self-image. He was of a diffident and timid personality and lacked those dynamic qualities we usually associate with leadership. Paul has to remind him that 'God did not give us a spirit of timidity, but a spirit of power, of love and of self-discipline' (2 Tim. 1:7). In addition, he seems to have suffered from indifferent health, and Paul advises him to 'stop drinking only water, and use a little wine because of your stomach and your frequent illnesses' (1 Tim. 5:23).

But the great thing is that, in spite of his personality problems and indifferent health, Timothy was mightily used of God, for he had the one thing that really matters—a deep love for the Lord Jesus Christ and his gospel.

People mentioned in 2 Timothy

LOIS, (1:5). Grandmother of Timothy and a Jewish Christian.

EUNICE, (1:5). Timothy's mother and also a Jewish Christian.

PHYGELUS AND HERMOGENES, (1:15). Two friends who accompanied Paul but deserted him in his hour of need. Nothing further is known about them.

ONESIPHORUS, (1:16). A friend who remained steadfast and visited Paul in prison.

HYMENAEUS AND PHILETUS, (2:17). Two leaders of the heretical movement in the church at Ephesus.

JANNES AND JAMBRES, (3:8). Neither is mentioned in the Old Testament but according to Jewish tradition they were the magicians who opposed Moses (Exod. 7:11).

DEMAS, (4:9). Once a fellow-worker with Paul and mentioned in Colossians 4:14 and Philemon 24. But he was seduced by a spirit of worldliness and deserted Paul.

CRESCENS, (4:10). A fellow-worker but mentioned only here in the New Testament.

TITUS, (4:10). One of Paul's young converts and a very capable leader who worked with the apostle in Ephesus, Corinth and Crete. Mentioned frequently in the epistles, one of which was written to him by Paul.

LUKE, (4:11). Author of the gospel named after him and also of Acts. He was a doctor (Col. 4:14) and a faithful friend and fellow-worker with Paul.

MARK, (4:11). Full name John Mark and author of the Gospel named after him. He had let Paul down on his first missionary journey (Acts 13:13), but later proved himself to Paul as a faithful worker.

TYCHICUS, (4:12). Described by Paul as a 'dear brother and faithful servant in the Lord' (Eph. 6:21). Almost certain that he carried Paul's letters to both Ephesus and Colosse.

Carpus, (4:13). Not mentioned elsewhere but must have been a close friend of Paul and had given him hospitality since the apostle had left both his cloak and parchments at his house in Troas.

ALEXANDER THE METALWORKER, (4:14-15). Possibly the same Alexander mentioned in 1 Timothy as a heretic alongside Hymenaeus. He strongly opposed Paul's message and did him a great deal of harm.

PRISCILLA AND AQUILA, (4:19). A godly husband and wife who were tent-makers like Paul, and gave him hospitality at

Corinth (Acts 18:1-3). They also helped the preacher, Apollos, to a clearer understanding of the gospel (Acts 18:24-26).

ERASTUS AND TROPHIMUS (4:20) were both co-workers with Paul and are mentioned respectively in Acts 19:22 and Acts 20:4.

EUBULUS, PUDENS, LINUS, AND CLAUDIA, (4:21). Nothing is known of these individuals and we must simply regard them as Christian believers in the church at Rome.

1 Fanning the flame of faith

(1:1-7)

As this letter is read and studied it will be helpful in getting a clearer understanding of it if one keeps in mind that this is a personal letter written to a very dear friend. Also, that it is—in a very real sense—Paul's last will and testament, since it was written during the last months before his death.

Persecution of the church was at its height under the Emperor Nero, and we should try to enter into Paul's feelings of loneliness and isolation as he awaits martyrdom in his cold prison cell.

The greeting

'Paul, an apostle of Christ Jesus by the will of God, according to the promise of life that is in Christ Jesus' (2 Tim. 1:1).

Although Timothy is a very dear friend, Paul is concerned at the outset to make it perfectly clear that this letter is not

simply 'a substitute for a friendly confidential chat'[1]. Hence
he begins by stressing his apostolic authority because he
wants Timothy to understand that he has some very serious
matters to bring to his attention as the pastor of the church in
Ephesus.

Paul always held a high view of his ministry as an apostle.
The meaning of 'apostle' is one 'sent on a mission', and in
Paul's case that mission was the preaching of the gospel. In
the opening verse of his letter to the Galatians he puts it even
more forcefully: 'Paul an apostle—sent not from men nor by
man, but by Jesus Christ and God the Father' (Gal. 1:1). His
apostleship was not a self-appointment, nor did he owe it to
the church, but it was solely by the will of God.

This note of authority is often lacking in the church today,
mainly because—in many instances—the Bible is no longer
given its proper and effective use in the pulpit. For the truth is
that it is through the witness of the prophets and apostles in
Scripture that the Word of God speaks. The preacher, who is
not content simply to give a religious lecture but faithfully
expounds the Bible, is therefore in the true apostolic
succession.

New life in Christ

Paul also says in this opening verse that the gospel he is
commissioned to preach is 'according to the promise of life
that is in Christ Jesus'. The remarkable thing is that it is
because of this gospel that he is facing death in his Roman
prison, and yet he has the assurance in his heart that the same
gospel promises him life in Christ. It brings us into the very

life of God himself. A new life-principle enters into the centre of our being as the Holy Spirit directs our hearts and minds, and enables us to interpret our human existence from God's view of things.

That is very different from the humanistic interpretation of life that is so prevalent today, and which Paul describes in Colossians as a 'hollow and deceptive philosophy, which depends on human tradition and the basic principles of this world rather than on Christ' (Col. 2:8). It is hollow and deceptive because it holds out a promise it cannot keep. We have only to look at our world with its violence, corruption, greed and discontent to see where this man-centred philosophy of life has really got us.

The apostolic blessing

'To Timothy, my dear son: Grace, mercy and peace from God the Father and Christ Jesus our Lord' (2 Tim. 1:2).

Much has already been said about Timothy in the introduction to this letter, and the only thing we need to emphasis again is the note of deep affection Paul had for the younger man. He is Paul's 'dear son' or 'dearly beloved son' (AV) because it was through the apostle's ministry that he was brought to birth in Christ. Any Christian who has been used of God in the conversion of another will be able to enter fully into Paul's feelings of warmth for Timothy, for there is no joy to be compared with that of winning someone for Christ.

In the apostolic blessing of 'grace, mercy, and peace', we have three great biblical words full of spiritual meaning.

Grace

This is the free, unmerited love of God extended to us in various ways. Common grace is God's providence in the gifts of his love to all mankind. Jesus put it like this: 'He causes his sun to rise on the evil and the good, and sends rain on the righteous and the unrighteous' (Matt. 5:45). That kind of love is not dependent on anything in man himself. It is free to all, and totally unmerited.

Keeping grace is the fresh supply of God's love and power to see us through the circumstances of each day. As John says, 'From the fulness of his grace we have all received one blessing after another' (John 1:16). In John Newton's memorable words,

Through many dangers, toils and snares
I have already come;
'Tis grace has brought me safe thus far,
And grace will lead me home.

Saving grace is the forgiveness of sins and the hope of eternal life through faith in Christ. We cannot save ourselves, or earn our salvation. We can only receive it as the free unmerited gift of God. 'For it is by grace you have been saved, through faith—and this not from yourselves, it is the gift of God—not by works, so that no one can boast (Eph. 2:8-9).

Mercy

All who have received the gift of salvation are the recipients of God's mercy. As Toplady's hymn says:

A debtor to mercy alone,
Of covenant mercy I sing;

But it is because we have received God's mercy that we in turn will show mercy to others. 'Blessed are the merciful,' said Jesus (Matt. 5:7). Mercy is an active, not a passive, state. It is not enough to feel merciful and compassionate to those in misery and suffering. We must deliberately bring our will into play by doing what we can to relieve that misery.

Christ's illustration of this is the parable of the Good Samaritan. The priest and the Levite may have felt pity for the man who was mugged on the Jericho road, but they did nothing about it! The Samaritan, on the other hand, showed he had experienced God's mercy by acting in a merciful way (Luke 10:25-37).

Peace

God's peace is a treasured possession but to have it we must first be reconciled to God, or be at peace *with* him instead of being alienated *from* him. Prior to conversion, a person is the enemy of God, and remains under God's wrath and judgement. That person's life, thoughts and feelings are all in opposition to God. 'The sinful mind is hostile to God. It does not submit to God's law, nor can it do so. Those controlled by the sinful nature cannot please God' (Rom. 8:7-8).

Through Christ's death on the cross to bear the judgement of our sin, we can be reconciled to God, and when that happens, we immediately begin to experience the gift of peace in our hearts. Our conscience is at rest, our relationship with God is settled, and the thought of judgement no longer disturbs us. We can sing with confidence:

We bless Thee for thy peace, O God,
Deep as the unfathomed sea,
Which falls like sunshine on the road
Of those who trust in Thee.

The value of a godly home

With the greeting at an end, Paul strikes the personal note which is the hallmark of this letter.

'I thank God, whom I serve, as my forefathers did, with a clear conscience, as night and day I constantly remember you in my prayers. Recalling your tears, I long to see you, so that I may be filled with joy' (2 Tim. 1:3-4).

The reference to his forefathers reminds us of the continuity between the old and new covenants, for Christ is the fulfilment of all the promises and prophecies of the Old Testament. This echoes his conversation with the disciples on the Emmaus road. 'And beginning with Moses and all the Prophets, he explained to them what was said in all the Scriptures concerning himself' (Luke 24:27). As for the tears Paul mentions, they were probably occasioned by his parting from Timothy for the last time. This was not simply emotionalism, but an indication of the depth of love we should have for one another as brothers and sisters in Christ.

But what really rejoices Paul's heart is the reminder of Timothy's faith, which owed so much to his spiritual upbringing.

'I have been reminded of your sincere faith, which first lived in your grandmother Lois and in your mother Eunice and, I am persuaded, now lives in you also' (2 Tim. 1:5).

Timothy was a third generation Christian and owed his 'sincere faith' to the groundwork done in his life by his mother and grandmother who had taught him the scriptures from infancy (2 Tim. 3:15). Throughout the Bible, the role of the family and godly parentage is clearly taught: 'Honour your father and your mother' (Exod. 20:12). 'Train a child in the way he should go, and when he is old he will not turn from it' (Prov. 22:6). 'Children obey your parents in the Lord, … Fathers, do not exasperate your children; instead, bring them up in the training and instruction of the Lord' (Eph. 6:1-4).

> The reference to his forefathers reminds us of the continuity between the old and new covenants, for Christ is the fulfilment of all the promises and prophecies of the Old Testament.

Being a parent in today's society is a difficult task, especially when there is no father to act as a role model as was true in Timothy's case. But God gives a special grace for the task as is evident from the good job Lois and Eunice did in bringing up Timothy who was to become a powerful advocate of the gospel and the pastor of the church at Ephesus.

Fanning the flame

Apart from his Christian upbringing Timothy also received a gift directly from God which made him the man he was.

'For this reason I remind you to fan into flame the gift of God, which is in you through the laying on of my hands. For

God did not give us a spirit of timidity, but a spirit of power, of love and of self-discipline' (2 Tim. 1:6-7).

Timothy's gift was probably associated with his having been set apart for the work of ministry through the laying on of hands by Paul and the elders of the church. But whatever the gift was, it arose out of his faith, as all God's gifts do. So when Paul urges him to 'fan into flame the gift of God', he is really saying something like this: 'Keep your faith and ministry alive, Timothy; do not let the demands of ministry and the responsibility of preaching the gospel in a pagan society get you down. Remember you are God's man, and the Spirit God has given you is not a Spirit of timidity, but 'of power, of love and of self-discipline'.'

Timothy's faith had not burnt out, but he needed this encouragement to fan it into a flame because of his fearful and sensitive temperament. He was not a born leader, and he had a tendency to shrink from the demands of ministry. Even his stomach complaint (1 Tim. 5:23) may have been a stress symptom.

The truth is that many of us need a bit of prodding from time to time to fan the flame of faith which can so easily lose its glow and vitality with the passage of time. To re-kindle it, we need to give more attention to prayer, and to the reading of God's Word, and to regular worship with God's people. And we are not alone in this, for we too have the Spirit of power, of love and of self-discipline.

FOR FURTHER STUDY

1. Look at other epistles where Paul begins by stressing his apostolic authority, especially Galatians. What are the main features of the authority of the apostles in the New Testament?

2. Try to find other passages in the Gospels and epistles where Jesus is spoken of as the fulfilment of the Old Testament.

TO THINK ABOUT AND DISCUSS

1. In prison, Paul was calm and serene, and able to speak of life although he was facing death. How should our faith help us to meet the difficulties of life?

2. Paul had a high view of his ministry as an apostle. We too should have a high view of our Christian calling. How should we express this in our day-to-day life?

3. Are we guilty at times of being too timid when it comes to witnessing for Christ? How does this passage fortify us in the area of sharing the gospel of Christ's grace with our fellow workers, family and friends?

4. What causes the flame of faith to burn low in the first place? Suggest ways and means by which we can fan the flame of faith when it burns low.

2 Not ashamed of the gospel

(1:8-18)

Paul is concerned to impress upon Timothy the glory of the gospel and the responsibility he has to be faithful to it in his ministry. Timothy should also be faithful to Paul, God's apostle, who in his imprisonment is suffering for the gospel and through whom the gift of faith had come to him. He must therefore be prepared, in spite of his natural timidity and weakness, to suffer with Paul for the gospel and never to be ashamed of it.

I t is inevitable that in the cause of Christ the Christian will encounter—at some time or other—opposition and hostility from the world. And when that happens, we may be tempted to distance ourselves from Christ and the gospel that saved us.

Testifying for Christ

'So do not be ashamed to testify about our Lord, or ashamed of me his prisoner (2 Tim. 1:8).

In the first place Paul describes himself not as a prisoner of the Roman emperor, but as the Lord's prisoner. He regarded his spell in a lonely prison cell as part of God's purpose for him, and was living up to what he had said earlier in his letter to the Romans. 'And we know that in all things God works for the good of those who love him, who have been called according to his purpose' (Rom. 8:28). Others had deserted him (v. 15) so he pleads with Timothy not to do the same by being ashamed of associating with him as a prisoner for the gospel.

We might think that if we have been truly born of the Holy Spirit that we have no need to be reminded not to be ashamed of testifying for Christ, or ashamed of the gospel of Christ or ashamed of the people of Christ. But it *does* happen. Peter denied Christ and his gospel not once, but three times! Phygelus and Hermogenes and others were ashamed to be associated with God's apostle and deserted the faith (2 Tim. 1:15). And there was Demas who 'loved this world' more than he loved Christ (2 Tim. 4:10).

We can also add to that the words of the Lord Jesus when he said: 'If anyone is ashamed of me and my words in this adulterous and sinful generation, the Son of Man will be ashamed of him when he comes in his Father's glory with the holy angels' (Mark 8:38). Such a warning would not have been necessary if the temptation to be ashamed of Christ and his gospel were not as real and common as it actually is.

But why should we ever be tempted to be ashamed of the gospel? Or, to put it in another way, why are we not sufficiently proud of it to want to testify to our faith in Christ to others? Is it because of our natural temperament? We are shy or timid like Timothy. But we are told that God has not given us a spirit of timidity, but of strength and power (2 Tim. 1:7). We can never allow temperament to prevent us from publicly owning Christ as our Saviour and Lord.

Or perhaps we are ashamed of the gospel because we value too highly the opinion of others; we fear ridicule because they may consider us old-fashioned or naïve. But should that matter? Is what others think of us to be regarded as more important than what God thinks of us?

The glory of the gospel

The apostle next sketches some of the main features of the gospel that make it so glorious, and so that Timothy will be proud to declare it in his ministry at Ephesus.

FIRST, it is the gospel of power, 'by the power of God, who has saved us and called us to a holy life' (2 Tim. 1:8-9). In our world today, people glory in their power which can take many different forms—military power, political power, technological power, economic power, etc. Indeed they are so obsessed with power that they think they can achieve almost anything in and of themselves, without help from any other source including God. And yet man's power, although great, is very limited when compared with the power of God for the following reasons. It is confined to this world only, for at some time each person has to die. It cannot permanently change human nature for the better, and it expresses itself in destruction rather than in salvation, hence the wars and violence that plague our world today.

But God's power affects not only life in this world, but in the eternal world through the resurrection of Jesus Christ.

Moreover, its purpose is not to destroy but to save. It saves us from sin and damnation and enables us to live a holy life that is beneficial for society and fits us for life in heaven. No other human message has the power to do these things, least of all so to change people on the inside that instead of living only to please themselves, they develop a concern for others and a desire to please God. That is a message our world sorely needs today, so why should we be ashamed of the gospel?

SECOND, it is the gospel of God's grace. '… God, who has saved us … not because of anything we have done but because of his own purpose and grace. This grace was given us in Christ Jesus before the beginning of time' (2 Tim. 1:9).

We have already seen, when considering Paul's greeting in verses 1 and 2, that grace is the free unmerited love of God. Whenever the New Testament says that God has done something by his grace, it means something we could never have done for ourselves, and which we do not deserve. But now the apostle adds something extra to the meaning of God's grace. He says that 'this grace was given us in Christ Jesus before the beginning of time'—a staggering thought. Our salvation did not begin with Christ's death and resurrection, nor when we put our faith in Christ as our Lord and Saviour. In fact, our salvation did not begin with anything that happened in this world and within the dimension of time. We must trace its source back to eternity when, before creation came into being, God had already laid down his plan and purpose to restore fallen sinners to a state of grace through Christ's atoning work on the cross. That is what makes our personal salvation the awe-inspiring experience it really is.

THIRD, it is the gospel of eternal life. '… But it has now been revealed through the appearing of our Saviour, Christ Jesus, who has destroyed death and has brought life and immortality to light through the gospel' (2 Tim. 1:10). Paul has already said that God's grace in salvation was conceived *before* the beginning of time. But now he is telling us that it was a plan that was revealed or made known to mankind *in time*, through the historical atoning death of Christ on the cross. In that atoning death, certain things followed.

Christ destroyed death. That does not mean that death was eliminated, since we see it happening all around us and all people are subject to it. But physical death, which is the separation of the soul from the body, is no longer a fearful prospect for the Christian, because Christ by his death and resurrection has made it ineffective and powerless. Jesus said, 'I am the resurrection and the life. He who believes in me will live, even though he dies; and whoever lives and believes in me will never die' (John 11:25-26). A further comforting thought is that Christ described death as a sleep. 'Our friend Lazarus has fallen asleep; but I am going there to wake him up' (John 11:11). And just as we wake up from sleep feeling refreshed, so in Christ we awake from death to the refreshing life of heaven.

But there is also spiritual death when the soul is 'dead in … transgressions and sins' (Eph. 2:1). But, through the saving work of Christ in the forgiveness of sins, that death has also been destroyed, and our souls have been made 'alive' (Eph. 2:4). And this new life, which is begun on earth, will one day come to its fulfilment in the eternal life in heaven.

Christ has also brought 'life and immortality to light through the gospel' (2 Tim. 1:10). By bringing these two terms 'life and immortality' together, Paul is saying that not only is the soul of the believer immortal, but the body will also become immortal on the resurrection morning. The classic passage on this great truth is in 1 Corinthians 15.

'Listen, I tell you a mystery: We will not all sleep, but we will all be changed—in a flash, in the twinkling of an eye, at the last trumpet. For the trumpet will sound, the dead will be raised imperishable, and we will be changed. For the perishable must clothe itself with the imperishable, and the mortal with immortality. When the perishable has been clothed with the imperishable, and the mortal with immortality, then the saying that is written will come true: "Death is swallowed up in victory" ' (1 Cor. 15:51-54).

Communicating the gospel

Having sketched the essential features of the gospel, Paul next reminds Timothy, and us, that we are under an obligation, as he was, to make the gospel known to others.

'And of this gospel I was appointed a herald and an apostle and a teacher. That is why I am suffering as I am. Yet I am not ashamed, because I know whom I have believed, and am convinced that he is able to guard what I have entrusted to him for that day' (2 Tim. 1:11-12).

If the gospel is as glorious as Paul has said it is, then Timothy should want above all else to make it known to others. Paul uses three terms to describe his own work in making it known—herald, apostle and teacher.

A herald was someone who proclaimed a message—and

that is the function of preachers today, to proclaim Christ and the message of salvation. This proclaiming of the gospel was so important to Paul that he was willing to suffer imprisonment for it, and he was certainly not ashamed to preach it because, as he says, 'I know whom I have believed, and am convinced that he is able to guard what I have entrusted to him for that day' (2 Tim. 1:12).

Not all bible commentators agree about what it was Paul had 'entrusted' to God's keeping. From the context it seems clear that it included both his own soul in salvation, and also the work of proclaiming that salvation to others. And that is true of us. We entrust our souls to God's keeping, and in the work of proclaiming Christ to others, whether as preachers or in our personal witness, we entrust that to him as well by asking his blessing upon it.

An apostle was a unique individual. There are no apostles today in the sense in which Paul uses the term. They were unique men whom Christ called, and to whom God revealed the gospel (Mark 3:13). The church is 'built on the foundation of the apostles and prophets' (Eph. 2:20). This

> **Preaching is mainly proclamation with a view to calling people to repentance and to faith in the Lord Jesus Christ. Teaching, on the other hand, is explaining the great truths and doctrines of Scripture, and the moral demands of the gospel, so that Christians can grow in their faith.**

then is the apostolic faith from which the church must not depart in her ministry to the world. The term 'teacher' is self-explanatory. And although the church today does not have apostles, she does have teachers. To a certain extent the functions of preaching and teaching overlap, but there is a difference between them. Preaching is mainly proclamation with a view to calling people to repentance and to faith in the Lord Jesus Christ. Teaching, on the other hand, is explaining the great truths and doctrines of Scripture, and the moral demands of the gospel, so that Christians can grow in their faith. Both are needed in the ministry of the local church.

Guarding the gospel

Timothy must not only communicate the gospel but he must guard it as a precious deposit. 'What you heard from me, keep as the pattern of sound teaching, with faith and love in Christ Jesus. Guard the good deposit that was entrusted to you—guard it with the help of the Holy Spirit who lives in us' (2 Tim. 1:13).

When we deposit money in the bank we are, in effect, saying: 'I am entrusting this treasure to your safe keeping—guard it for me'. In the deposit of the gospel, Paul had laid down the pattern of sound teaching to be followed, and Timothy was not to depart from it. To be a true Christian is to be a guardian of God's Word, to defend its authority and truthfulness, and not to dilute or distort its message to suit popular thinking. Paul lays great emphasis upon this elsewhere. 'We do not use deception, nor do we distort the word of God. On the contrary, by setting forth the truth plainly we commend ourselves to every man's conscience in the sight of God' (2 Cor. 4:2).

Timothy would have his work cut out to guard the gospel, because there were those in Ephesus who would seek to corrupt it, just as there are those in the church today who undermine the truth of Scripture. But he would not be alone in this, and neither are we. We can do it 'with the help of the Holy Spirit who lives in us' (2 Tim. 1:14).

Onesiphorus, a refreshing character

Try to imagine Paul's situation. He feels lonely and isolated in his cold prison cell. 'You know that everyone in the province of Asia has deserted me, including Phygelus and Hermogenes' (2 Tim. 1:15). We know nothing of these two men, but the implication is that they had once been close to him, and now in his hour of need they had repudiated him.

How uplifting and refreshing to Paul's spirit therefore to have a lovely, winsome character like Onesiphorus to visit him in his prison cell. 'May the Lord show mercy to the household of Onesiphorus, because he often refreshed me and was not ashamed of my chains. On the contrary, when he was in Rome, he searched hard for me until he found me. May the Lord grant that he will find mercy from the Lord on that day!' (2 Tim. 1:16-18).

The name Onesiphorus means 'profitable' and he was certainly that to Paul, both as a fellow-believer and as a Christian friend. Paul says, 'When he was in Rome, he searched hard for me until he found me'. This gracious man went to great trouble on the apostle's behalf. He had not a clue where Paul was incarcerated, but day after day with grim determination he roamed the streets of the city, asking questions and gleaning every bit of information he could, until eventually he found Paul in his prison cell and was able to refresh him in his soul and spirit.

There are people in the church in whose company we feel drained and empty, but there are others who brace us up and come like a breath of fresh air into our lives. Onesiphorus was like that. And it seems he carried out a similar ministry of refreshment in the church at Ephesus. Paul says, 'You know very well in how many ways he helped me in Ephesus' (2 Tim. 1:18).

And we can exercise that refreshing ministry if we have a mind to, since it does not call for any special talent or training. How do we do it? By getting alongside people in their distresses and so refreshing them in their spirit by showing kindness and compassion. Also we do it by giving encouragement to others. Eliphaz, a friend of Job, said to him: 'Your words have supported those who stumbled; you have strengthened faltering knees' (Job 4:4). There must be many other ways in which we can bring refreshment of spirit into people's lives. May God help us to get on with it.

For further study ▶

FOR FURTHER STUDY

1. Read through Acts and see how many people you can discover who suffered for the gospel like Paul.

2. Read 1 Corinthians 15 and learn all you can about the death and resurrection of the Christian, especially the resurrection of the body. Also look up other passages which help to explain what the resurrection body will be like, e.g. Mark 12:24-27.

TO THINK ABOUT AND DISCUSS

1. Paul urges Timothy not to be ashamed of the gospel but to suffer for it. How does this apply to Christians today, and what part does our natural temperament play in this?

2. Paul mentions three of the main features of the gospel—power, grace and eternal life. Discuss and explain what you consider to be outstanding features of the gospel.

3. We cannot deny that modern society has enormous power through its knowledge, science and technology. But how does this fall short of God's power, and what are its limitations?

4. Paul's statement that salvation came to us 'before the beginning of time' raises deep questions about predestination and election. Read Ephesians 1:1-12 and discuss the passage to see what you can learn about this teaching.

5. Consider the example of Onesiphorus. What other ways, apart from those specifically mentioned, can we exercise a ministry of refreshment like he did?

3 Transmitting the Word

(2:1-7)

Towards the close of the first chapter Paul, expressed his disappointment that the Christian brethren in Asia, including Phygelus and Hermogenes, had deserted both him and the cause of Christ. The one outstanding exception had been Onesiphorus who had remained faithful to the gospel and to Paul by visiting him in prison.

It is against this background of a general falling away that this chapter opens with the apostle urging Timothy not to follow the example of the deserters, but to stand his ground and not to let his natural timidity betray him into disloyalty.

Strong in the Lord

'You then, my son, be strong in the grace that is in Christ Jesus' (2 Tim. 2:1).

Timothy may be weak and timid in himself, but he is to

find his strength and power for service not in himself alone but in the grace that God supplies. God's grace saves us and it keeps us, but it also provides us with the inward motivation and strength to carry on God's work, even when we feel like giving up.

John Wesley provides a good example. He travelled the roads of England on horseback for fifty years as a messenger of the heavenly King. He would preach five or six times on each day's journey, was in danger from highwaymen, was attacked by angry mobs, was always poor, and had the pulpits of the established church closed against him. Physically he was a small, weak man, but nothing could deter him from carrying out the Lord's work. He really was the 'Knight of the Burning Heart' as Leslie Church once called him. In the words of Nehemiah, it could be said of him , 'the joy of the Lord is your strength' (Neh. 8:10).

And our strength in the Lord's work comes from the same source, and not from our own ability alone.

Passing on the Word

Timothy has already been urged to guard the deposit of truth which he has received from Paul, and also to be strong in preaching that truth in the face of any opposition he might encounter in his ministry at Ephesus. But now the apostle goes a step further and urges him to arrange for the transmission of the truth of the gospel to the next generation.

'And the things you have heard me say in the presence of many witnesses entrust to reliable men who will also be qualified to teach others' (2 Tim. 2:2).

Paul knows that his end is near and that execution awaits him. He has carried the torch of the gospel over many years, and he is now concerned that it should be handed on to others to carry it forward. There is, as it were, a chain of transmission by which the revelation of God's truth in the Scriptures has come down to us. In our present instance it began when God revealed the gospel through Christ to Paul when he first became an apostle. Speaking of that experience, he says distinctly: 'I did not receive it from any man, nor was I taught it; rather, I received it by revelation from Jesus Christ' (Gal. 1:12). Having received it, he now says he has passed it on to Timothy in 'the things you have heard me say in the presence of many witnesses'. Timothy must now train reliable men from among his people at Ephesus who are qualified to become another link in the chain by teaching the gospel to others.

We have a similar chain of transmission in Revelation 1:1. 'The revelation of Jesus Christ, which God gave him... He made it known by sending his angel to his servant John, who testifies to everything he saw—that is, the word of God and the testimony of Jesus Christ.' The word of truth comes from God through Christ to John, who, in turn, wrote it down for the benefit of the church.

The men Timothy is to train for future ministry must be 'qualified to teach' (2 Tim. 2:2). Paul stressed the same facility for ministry in 1 Timothy 3:2—'the overseer must be... able to teach.' He will also mention it again in verse 24 of 2 Timothy 2. Why this emphasis? Because a man may have other gifts of leadership in the church, but if he does not have the ability to expound the doctrines of Scripture, and be able to communicate those truths in a way people can understand, then he has no place in the preaching ministry. Sadly, this piece of apostolic counsel is all too often ignored in the church today, and there are men in the pastoral office who see themselves first and foremost, not as preachers, but as administrators, counsellors, and social engineers.

Metaphors of ministry

If a pastor is faithful in his calling to preach the Word of God without fear or favour, he will find it a hard task at times. This was especially true for Timothy when the hardship would involve physical persecution. But even today, the evangelical pastor can find himself in a very lonely position because of his stand on biblical authority. Furthermore, this is a problem that might well become more acute in the future because of increasing secularization and growing hostility to the Word of God. Paul now enlarges on this aspect of the pastoral ministry with the use of three vivid images—the soldier, the athlete, and the farmer.

The soldier

'Endure hardship with us like a good soldier of Christ Jesus. No one serving as a soldier gets involved in civilian affairs— he wants to please his commanding officer' 2 Tim. 2: 3-4).

Soldiering can be tough at times, but it can also bring its own rewards. So it is with ministry. Like a soldier on active service, the Christian pastor is in the forefront of the spiritual warfare that rages in the world between the forces of truth and righteousness and the powers of darkness and falsehood. He will devote himself therefore to pleasing his Lord in the same way as the soldier concentrates on his soldiering in order to please his commanding officer.

Furthermore, just as the soldier is called to be a soldier and not to get involved in civilian affairs, so the pastor must give himself essentially to the work of pastoring, and not get so tied up with secular matters that they hinder him from fruitful study of God's Word and the care of souls.

Commenting on this passage, John Stott says, '... this needs to be remembered in our day when 'auxiliary', 'supplementary', and 'part-time' ministries are increasing in which the pastor continues his trade or profession, and exercises his ministry in his spare time. Such ministries can hardly be said to contravene scripture. Yet they are difficult to reconcile with the apostle's injunction to avoid entanglements.'[2]

The athlete

'Similarly, if anyone competes as an athlete, he does not receive the victor's crown unless he competes according the rules' (2 Tim. 2:5).

When it comes to the discipline, integrity, and dedication of the Christian life, the picture of the athlete is very appropriate. Paul is probably thinking of the Greek games—the Olympics—which had their own rules just as sports do today. Today, much is said about the use of drugs in sport, which in effect is breaking the rules. As a result, some athletes have had to return the medal (victor's crown) they had won—but won by cheating.

For the Christian, there are rules and principles to be observed in daily living. The moral law of the gospel is given to us as a guide for our behaviour. We are in the world, but we are not to be part of it because we follow a different code of conduct. If we fail in seeking to live a holy life, then we have no right to expect God to bless us, or to see our Christian life flourish. This applies especially to the pastor's ministry. He must obey the rules in preaching the eternal truths of the gospel, and not be content simply to express his own opinions on the problems facing the world.

The farmer

'The hardworking farmer should be the first to receive a share of the crops' (2 Tim. 2:6).

The image here is not of the man who enjoys working in his allotment or garden as a hobby on summer evenings. It pictures the 'hardworking farmer'—the man who toils and labours without any thought of the glamour and medals associated with the soldier and the athlete. In Psalm 126, there is a picture of the painful anxious care with which the farmer of ancient times sowed the seed.

'Those who sow in tears
   will reap with songs of joy.
He who goes out weeping,
   carrying seed to sow,
will return with songs of joy,
   carrying sheaves with him' (vv. 5-6).

This is still true today for those in third world countries where mechanization has not yet been introduced to agriculture. The peasant farmer has to toil endlessly with primitive tools if he or she is to get a share of the crop. The main point of the illustration is all too clear. The Christian cannot expect a fruitful spiritual life without perseverance and effort. In the following quotation, J C Ryle uses the colourful phrase, 'no gain without pain'.

'I will never shrink from declaring my belief that there are no spiritual gains without pains. I should as soon expect a farmer to prosper in business who concerned himself with sowing his fields and never looking at them till harvest, as expect a believer to attain to holiness who was not diligent about his Bible reading, his prayers, and the use of his Sunday. Our God is a God who works by means, and He will never bless the soul of that man who pretends to be so high and spiritual that he can get on without them'.3

The image here ... pictures the 'hardworking farmer'—the man who toils and labours without any thought of the glamour and medals associated with the soldier and the athlete.

Reflection on the Word

This first section of the chapter ends with the apostle urging Timothy to think deeply about what he has been teaching him.

'Reflect on what I am saying, for the Lord will give you insight into all this' (2 Tim. 2:7).

In effect Paul is saying: 'Take seriously what I am teaching you, Timothy, for it is not merely a human word, but as God's apostle I am bringing you the word of God.' It reminds us of the words Jesus often used when concluding his parables, 'He, who has ears to hear, let him hear.' We can be guilty of hearing God's Word preached, or read from the Scriptures, but without really reflecting on it so as to get insight into its meaning and application to our own lives.

Sad to say, there are Christians who never get down to any serious Bible study, but are content with the kind of devotional reading that never really stretches their minds. God never bypasses the mind and the mental struggle involved in getting to grips with the truth of his Word. Ministers especially should give themselves to in-depth study of God's Word, digging deeply into the text so as to gain insight into its meaning and message for the benefit of their people. At the same time, care should be taken not to make it simply an intellectual exercise, but to accompany it with prayer for the illumination which only the Holy Spirit can give.

FOR FURTHER STUDY

1. Paul uses military imagery in Ephesians 6:10-20. Study this passage to see what it says about the enemies of the gospel and how we are to equip ourselves for the spiritual warfare.

2. Timothy is urged to 'endure hardship' (v. 3). Read 2 Corinthians 11:21-29 and Acts 16:16-24 to learn about the hardships Paul himself went through.

3. Transmitting the gospel is not only for preachers. Read John 1:35-49 and Acts 9:4-8 to see how ordinary Christians can transmit the gospel to others.

TO THINK ABOUT AND DISCUSS

1. What are the things that will help us to be 'strong in the grace of Christ'? What does Paul mean when he says, 'For when I am weak, then I am strong' (2 Cor. 12:10)?

2. Timothy is to choose men 'qualified to teach' God's Word. What do you think those qualifications are? Is the preaching ministry still important today? What could you do in your church to help promote and encourage biblical preaching to take place? How could you encourage others to listen more carefully to sermons?

3. Using the three metaphors of the soldier, the athlete and the farmer, add your own thoughts and discuss how these images apply to the life of the Christian. What are the particular opportunities and difficulties each is likely to face?

4. Do you agree with the quotation of John Stott on his view of ministry when referring to the metaphor of the soldier? Why or why not?

4 Things worth remembering

(2:8-13)

From the outset of this letter, Paul has been concerned to encourage and inspire Timothy in his work as the pastor of the church at Ephesus. These were difficult times for Christian believers; persecution was widespread, and heresy in the church was on the increase.

By way of encouragement, Paul has already reminded Timothy of his godly upbringing and his ordination by the laying on of hands, and he has illustrated the task of the ministry with reference to the warfare of the soldier, the discipline of the athlete, and the hard work of the farmer.

A new section now commences, beginning at verse 8, in which Paul continues with the same theme by making an even more powerful appeal to Timothy to remain strong in his faith and in the work of the gospel.

The need to remember

'Remember Jesus Christ, raised from the dead, descended from David. This is my gospel for which I am suffering even to the point of being chained like a criminal. But God's word is not chained' (2 Tim. 2:8-9).

We may think that it was totally unnecessary for Paul to have to remind Timothy to 'remember Jesus Christ', as if there was any likelihood that he would ever forget! But if Timothy was anything like the rest of us, and I suspect he was, then he was rather prone to forget. For the truth is that human memory is erratic, and even the most precious experience can fade from our minds with the passage of time. Paul was really emphasizing that Timothy should make a conscious effort to keep the awareness of Christ in the forefront of his thinking, and not allow all the other experiences that crowded his life to squeeze out the greatest experience of all which was his indebtedness to Christ for the gift of salvation.

The same applies to us. Was not that the reason why Christ instituted the communion service for the church? Did not he say that we were to observe in the symbols of bread and wine the remembrance of his body given, and his blood shed, for the remission of our sins? It is not that we are so much in danger of forgetting Christ altogether, but that, with the passing of time, the memory of our conversion can lose its edge and no longer grip us with the sense of wonder, love and praise that we experienced at the first.

Perhaps it would help us to keep that memory fresh and alive if we were to sing in every service a hymn like the following:

King of my life I crown you now,
Yours shall the glory be;
Lest I forget your thorn-crowned brow,
Lead me to Calvary.

Lest I forget Gethsemane,
Lest I forget your agony,
Lest I forget your love for me,
Lead me to Calvary.

There are many things we need to remember concerning the Lord Jesus Christ, but Paul mentions three in particular that he wants Timothy to keep in the forefront of his thinking.

Christ risen

In the first place, Timothy is to remember Jesus Christ 'raised from the dead', not only as an objective reality, but also as a living, continuing presence in his daily life. From the historical standpoint, the resurrection of Christ was to become the cornerstone in the preaching ministry of the early church. If the story of Jesus had ended with his crucifixion, then the victory would have been with men and the powers of darkness in the world. However, the last word is never with men but always with God, as the resurrection was to testify. Writing to the Corinthians, Paul says that without the resurrection the Christian message is emptied of its essential content. 'And if Christ has not been raised, our preaching is useless and so is your faith' (1 Cor. 15:14).

We need to be told this today for there is a tendency in some quarters of the church to play down the bodily resurrection of Christ in the mistaken belief that it will make the gospel message more acceptable to modern scientific thinking. But that means we no longer have a gospel or good news to preach but only a humanistic philosophy. The gospel is good news precisely because it *is* the supernatural power of God manifested in the bodily resurrection of Jesus Christ. That is the historical reality.

But equally important is the present reality of knowing the power of the resurrection here and now. From the political perspective, our world is balanced on a knife-edge with its constant wars, global pollution and widespread hunger and poverty. To live victoriously in a world like that, and to overcome the ravages of sin, we need the power and inner reinforcement that the spirit of the risen Christ brings into our lives.

> Writing to the Corinthians, Paul says that without the resurrection the Christian message is emptied of its essential content.

Christ descended from David

Timothy is to remember Jesus Christ 'descended from David'. He was the God-Man, both Son of God and Son of Man, perfect in his divinity as the risen and ascended Lord, and also perfect in his humanity as descended from the line of David. In Philippians it is recorded that he, 'being in very nature God, did not consider equality with God something to be grasped, but made himself nothing, taking the very nature of a servant, being made in human likeness' (Phil. 2:6-7).

The significance of such a passage is that it tells us that our Saviour lived a human, earthly life with all its struggles and pressures, and therefore he knows and understands our humanity, and the pressures we are under in seeking to live the Christian life in today's world. The writer to the Hebrews says: 'For we do not have a high priest who is unable to sympathize with our weaknesses, but we have one who has been tempted in every way, just as we are—yet was without sin' (Heb. 4:15). The same truth is expressed very powerfully in Henry Twell's hymn:

> O Saviour Christ Thou too art Man;
> Thou hast been troubled, tempted, tried;
> Thy kind but searching glance can scan
> The very wounds that shame would hide.

It is a great encouragement and inspiration to realize that the Saviour knows our hopes and fears, our longings and aspirations after holiness, our failures and defeats, and that, in it all, he still loves us and intends at the last to bring us into the heavenly home.

Christ's gospel

Timothy must also remember that the incarnation and resurrection of Christ is the very heart of the gospel he is called upon to preach. 'Remember Jesus Christ, raised from the dead, descended from David. This is my gospel, for which I am suffering even to the point of being chained like a criminal. But God's word is not chained'. (2 Tim. 2:8-9). It is by these truths that people are saved and reconciled to God, and no amount of suffering or unpopularity Timothy may have to encounter should prevent him preaching that gospel.

Paul himself was having to suffer the painful indignity of suffering in chains like a common criminal, but it was worth it in order that God's elect 'may obtain the salvation that is in Christ Jesus, with eternal glory' (2 Tim. 2:10).

The preacher of today is under the same obligation to preach the same gospel, whatever indignity or unpopularity it may involve. He must not be unduly concerned to please people, or to shape his message to suit the thinking of the day. He must remain faithful to the revelation given and not distort in any way its substance. Paul reinforces this truth by quoting in part what is generally agreed among Bible scholars to be an early Christian hymn.

A trustworthy saying

Here is a trustworthy saying:
If we died with him,
   we will also live with him;
if we endure,
   we will also reign with him.
If we disown him,
   he will also disown us;
If we are faithless,
   he will remain faithful,
   for he cannot disown himself (2 Tim. 2:11-13).

Here are the positive and negative aspects of Christian experience. The first two parts refer to those who are true and faithful; the second two parts refer to those who are false and faithless.

The faithful

'If we died with him; we will also live with him.' This can be the experience of the Christian in two ways. First, in the early church believers faced death and martyrdom in the certain conviction that they would live with Christ in glory. Paul himself was expecting martyrdom after his imprisonment, and in parts of the world today, Christians are dying for the gospel. Second, there is another kind of dying—a dying to self. When we belong to Christ, we die to the claims of the world, and to the claims our own love of ease and comfort make upon us. We desire first and foremost to live for Christ and with Christ.

'If we endure, we will also reign with him.' Being a Christian has never been easy, and today it can still be something of an endurance test. Nothing in our society encourages a person to live for Christ and to seek to live a holy life. On the contrary, the opposite is true. Ours is a soft, flabby society which is superficial, loves to be entertained, lacks seriousness about eternal values, and is cushioned against any kind of endurance and self-sacrifice. But if, in spite of that prevailing attitude, we remain faithful to our spiritual convictions and endure with Christ, then we shall one day reign with him in glory. That is what Christ meant when he said, 'Blessed are the meek, for they shall inherit the earth' (Matt. 5:5). That is, at Christ's return in glory, we shall reign with him in the new heaven and the new earth.

The faithless

'If we disown him, he will also disown us.' That may sound

harsh, but the statement is quite categorical and actually repeats Christ's own words: 'Whoever acknowledges me before men, I will also acknowledge him before my Father in heaven. But whoever disowns me before men, I will disown him before my Father in heaven' (Matt. 10:32-33). That is a dreadful possibility to contemplate, but what comes next is even more fearful.

'If we are faithless, he will remain faithful, for he cannot disown himself' (2 Tim. 2:13). This statement is sometimes misunderstood, and is taken to be a statement of comfort—meaning that even when we turn from Christ he will never turn away from us. But it cannot possibly mean that, since Christ has already said that he will disown us if we disown him! The statement therefore is a grave warning that Christ will be faithful in carrying out his threat. As Hendiksen puts it: 'Faithfulness on his part means carrying out his threats as well as his promises'4. That must be so, for God cannot disown his own word.

Let us then take the warning to heart and remain faithful to Christ, for no price is too great to pay for the hope that one day we shall reign with him in heaven.

For further study ▶

FOR FURTHER STUDY

1. Look up those passages in the Gospels where the humanity of Jesus is evident, and also those passages where his divine nature is most prominent.

2. The resurrection was the keystone in the preaching of the early church. Read through Acts and make a list of the number of times it is referred to, and the degree of detail in which it is described. How does this compare with preaching on the resurrection you have heard in your church?

TO THINK ABOUT AND DISCUSS

1. How important is the use of one's memory when it comes to matters of spiritual experience? Do you agree that, with the passage of time, we can forget the most precious experiences—even our conversion? How might we prevent that from happening?

2. How important is the communion service? In some churches it is held every Sunday, in others twice a month, in still others four times a year. How often do you think it should be held?

3. Was Paul right to say (1 Cor. 15:14) that without the resurrection of Jesus, preaching and faith are empty and useless?

4. Some people stress the humanity of Jesus, for it makes them feel closer to him. Emphasizing his divinity, they say, can make him seem too remote. What do you think?

5 A workman approved of God

(2:14-26)

In the last chapter, Paul was concerned to remind Timothy of those basic truths that underlie the gospel, and to which he must remain faithful in his preaching ministry at Ephesus. 'Remember Jesus Christ, raised from the dead, descended from David. This is my gospel…' (2 Tim. 2:8-9). Now in the same way Timothy, in turn, must remind his own people of 'these things', especially those men he regards as 'qualified to teach others' (2 Tim. 2:2).

Empty words

'**K**eep reminding them of these things. Warn them before God against quarrelling about words; it is of no value, and only ruins those who listen' (2 Tim. 2:14).

The warning against disputing about mere words, and wasting time in hair-splitting arguments, is repeated in verse 16 where Paul describes it as 'godless chatter'. He clearly had in mind certain people in Ephesus who liked to play with religious ideas and words in the way that a small boy plays a game of marbles. They speculated about God and wove high-sounding theories about Christianity until they reduced it to some kind of meaningless and vague philosophy.

We still have to contend with a similar kind of thing today; you can meet such people in the church. They spend a lot of time talking and arguing about the Christian faith instead of living it. They are not really soul-searching for the truth, but are toying with the gospel, speculating about marginal issues which do not help themselves or others to grow in faith.

Dr Johnson was a great conversationalist and described himself as, 'a man who loves to fold his legs and have his talk out'. For that reason he could not understand the sense of purpose and commitment that drove John Wesley. He said to Boswell on one occasion, 'I hate to meet with John Wesley, the dog enchants me with his conversation, and then breaks off to go and visit some old woman'5. Johnson was a man of talk, but Wesley was a man of talk and action, and helped to change the face of England for the kingdom of God.

There are also those in our churches, who may not be great talkers, but they are forever getting caught up in the latest fad or novelty on the Christian scene, instead of getting down to some solid Bible study that will inform their minds and deepen their understanding of those essential truths of which Paul reminds Timothy.

The good and bad workman

'Do your best to present yourself to God as one approved, a

workman who does not need to be ashamed and who correctly handles the word of truth' (2 Tim. 2:15).

Here Paul is urging Timothy to see himself as a good workman for God. In ministry, the difference between the good and bad workman is that the former wants the approval of God upon his work, whereas the latter wants the approval of men. Timothy will have God's approval and blessing on his preaching and teaching if he 'correctly handles the word of truth' and has no 'need to be ashamed' of his ministry.

The word of truth for today's Christian workman is the revelation of God in Scripture which he will handle correctly, not deviating from its teaching, nor distorting its message in any way. The preacher is not in the pulpit to dispense his own opinions about the state of the world, or how the members of his congregation might make themselves better people. He is God's workman, and the work given him is to preach the unadulterated truth of the Word

> In ministry, the difference between the good and bad workman is that the former wants the approval of God upon his work, whereas the latter wants the approval of men.

of God with a view to the conversion of sinners, and the deepening of people's faith.

Paul next turns to the bad workmen and cites as an example Hymenaeus and Philetus.

'Avoid godless chatter, because those who indulge in it will become more and more ungodly. Their teaching will spread like gangrene. Among them are Hymenaeus and Philetus, who have wandered away from the truth' (2 Tim. 2:16-18).

Here were two heretics who had forfeited God's approval because they were engaged in empty 'godless chatter', and had undermined the truth of God's Word. Like some gangrenous disease, their false teaching was spreading like a poison, corrupting and infecting the minds and hearts of the people in their understanding of the wholesome gospel.

What was their heresy? 'They say that the resurrection has already taken place, and they destroy the faith of some'. (2 Tim. 2:18). We must be clear what Hymenaeus and Philetus were in fact teaching. They were not denying the resurrection of Jesus, but were saying that the resurrection of the Christian occurred when a person was baptized and rose into new spiritual life. But that was to deny one of the essential beliefs of the Christian faith, namely the physical resurrection of the body. Paul puts it very clearly in 1 Corinthians. 'So will it be with the resurrection of the dead. The body that is sown is perishable, it is raised imperishable; it is sown in dishonour, it is raised in glory; it is sown in weakness, it is raised in power; it is sown a natural body, it is raised a spiritual body' (1 Cor. 15:42-44).

What Timothy is being told about the good and bad workman echoes what Jesus taught about the good and bad shepherd in John 10. The good shepherd leads the flock out to pasture and feeds them and cares for them. The bad shepherd is the hired hand who is not really interested in the welfare of the flock, and when the wolf comes, flees and leaves the sheep to their fate. The pastor who 'correctly handles the word of truth' has a deep concern for the welfare of the souls in his charge. The pastor who distorts that word and undermines its basic doctrines is abandoning the sheep and leaving them to their spiritual fate.

The solid foundation

Although error is being taught and promulgated in today's church, and people's faith is being seriously undermined, does that mean that the true church of God will ultimately be destroyed? The answer Paul gives to that is a resounding 'No'.

'Nevertheless, God's solid foundation stands firm, sealed with this inscription: "The Lord knows those who are his", and, "Everyone who confesses the name of the Lord must turn away from wickedness" ' (2 Tim. 2:19).

By 'God's solid foundation' Paul has in mind the true church which consists of all those who confess the name of the Lord Jesus Christ as Saviour and have turned from wickedness to a holy life.

That church will never be destroyed, however much it is plagued by the poisonous teaching of men like Hymenaeus and Philetus. That church will stand and be triumphant as Jesus promised. 'I will build my church, and the gates of Hades [hell] will not overcome it' (Matt. 16:18). We must imagine the gates of hell being thrown wide open and all the demonic forces led by Satan himself rushing out to destroy and batter down the witness of the true church, only to fail because it is built on the solid foundation of God's truth.

On that foundation is written the twofold description: 'The Lord knows those who are his', and, 'Everyone who confesses the name of the Lord must turn away from wickedness' (2 Tim. 2:19). In the final analysis, the Lord alone knows the state of the heart, and can tell who truly belongs to him, and who those are who hold a spurious confession. But from the human perspective we ourselves are able to recognize those who belong to Christ by their holiness of life.

Members of God's household

In this final section, beginning at verse 20, Paul is still talking about the church, but he now uses the metaphor of a large house with its contents.

'In a large house there are articles not only of gold and silver, but also of wood and clay; some are for noble purposes and some for ignoble. If a man cleanses himself from the latter, he will be an instrument for noble purposes, made holy, useful to the Master and prepared to do any good work' (2 Tim. 2:20-21).

Remember this is only a metaphor, and as with all metaphors we must not press it too far. But the point Paul is making is perfectly clear. The articles of gold and silver could be for personal use and used for special (noble) occasions. The cheaper articles of wood and earthenware—perhaps for use in the kitchen—have a more menial (ignoble) use. Similarly, the church, God's house on earth, is a mixed company of true believers, comparable to gold and silver, and nominal believers, comparable to wood and earthenware.

The message is, if we want to be an instrument for noble purpose in God's household, we must keep ourselves from the polluting influences that can infect the church through false teaching and from the influences of those spurious members who know nothing of God's salvation in Christ. Instead, we will desire to be 'made holy', to love God's word and prayer, and to be useful in the Master's service.

Leaders in God's household

What is true of the members of the church is also true of its pastors and leaders. There are true leaders like Timothy, and false leaders like Hymenaeus and Philetus. Timothy is to 'flee the evil desires of youth, and pursue righteousness, faith, love and peace, along with those who call on the Lord out of a pure heart' (2 Tim. 2:22). By 'evil desires of youth' is not meant necessarily wrong sexual desires, although it could be that. It refers to sinful desires in general, and this could mean—for the spiritual leader—the love of money, the love of power, self-assertion and overriding ambition. Instead of being motivated by these desires, a minister, if he wants to gain the love and respect of his people, must pursue a life that is godly and peaceable.

Furthermore, the spiritual leader is to give special attention to his role as preacher and teacher.

'Don't have anything to do with foolish and stupid arguments, because you know they produce quarrels. And the Lord's servant must not quarrel; instead, he must be kind to everyone, able to teach, not resentful. Those who oppose him he must gently instruct, in the hope that God will grant them repentance leading them to a knowledge of the truth, and that they will come to their senses and escape from the trap of the devil, who has taken them captive to do his will' (2 Tim. 2:23-26).

The pastor is to avoid wasting his valuable time in useless

controversy with those who are awkward and of an unteachable spirit, for it only leads to dissension. Instead, he must give himself to the positive side of his ministry which is to teach those committed to his care. At times, there will be some who may oppose his teaching, but even then he will be positive in the manner he deals with them. He will be patient, not taking offence, and will try, in a gracious manner, to correct their wrong thinking, and bring them to 'repentance' and 'knowledge of the truth'.

In all this, the pastor will remind himself that he is not only dealing with people, but is encountering 'the trap of the devil' who has taken them 'captive to do his will'. This is the greatest challenge of all to a faithful ministry. Behind the scenes, Satan himself is at work manipulating, scheming, and seducing the hearts and minds of men and women. As Paul writes to the Ephesians when speaking of the warfare of the Spirit, he says, 'Our struggle is not against flesh and blood, but against the rulers, against the authorities, against the powers of this dark world and against the spiritual forces of evil in the heavenly realms' (Eph. 6:12).

Only that pastor, who is endued with the Spirit of God, and who stands firm on the Word of truth, can bring deliverance to those who are captive to the devil's will.

Characterization of godlessness

Paul next describes the kind of people who will be responsible for the godlessness of these 'terrible times'.

'People will be lovers of themselves, lovers of money, boastful, proud, abusive, disobedient to their parents, ungrateful, unholy, without love, unforgiving, slanderous, without self-control, brutal, not lovers of the good, treacherous, rash, conceited, lovers of pleasure rather than lovers of God—having a form of godliness but denying its power. Have nothing to do with them' (2 Tim. 3:2-5).

> This means that we in today's church have to be realistic and not expect the Christian life to get any easier, but accept that ours is a fallen world and that such distress and 'terrible times' might yet come even in our own country.

Here is a description of the moral deterioration that occurs in society when godlessness is its main feature. In Romans 1, Paul indicates that godlessness always precedes wickedness. 'The wrath of God is being revealed from heaven against all the godlessness and wickedness of men who suppress the truth by their wickedness (Rom. 1:18). And the list of sins given in 2 Tim. 3:2-5 begins with people who are 'lovers of themselves', and ends by saying they are not 'lovers of God'. In between come all the other vicious qualities.

We do not have to deal with each of these sins individually to see that if a person is driven by self-love at the outset, then all the other sins follow quite naturally. For when self is on the throne of the personality, then love for God and other people is of little consequence. Thus the list describes not only the breakdown in morals, but also the breakdown in human relationships within the family (parents and children), and in anti-social behaviour (lacking self-control, brutal, haters of the good). In addition, the godless society is materialistic, and governed by the senses in hot pursuit of pleasure and prosperity (lovers of money and lovers of pleasure).

It may well be that the church in western nations is now living through one of these 'terrible times' Paul is describing. Certainly the sins mentioned are all very much to the forefront in today's society. In his book *Holiness and the Spirit of the Age*,7 Floyd McClung writes:

> We live in a complex world and are surrounded by an ungodly culture. German sociologist Max Webber suggests that modern culture is like a beautiful, gilded bird cage. We are caught in it and we cannot escape. We are encircled by its ideas and ideologies, by its structures and systems. Our culture is essentially unsympathetic—sometimes even hostile—to all we are called to be and to do as Christians.

We may indeed wish at times to escape the godless culture of the world, but in the high-priestly prayer Jesus prayed for his followers, we read: 'My prayer is not that you take them out of the world but that you protect them from the evil one' (John 17:15). We must be determined therefore not to be seduced by Satan and the false glamour of the secular society.

Formal religion

The most shocking aspect of this picture Paul is describing is that these godless people are actually to be found within the visible church—'having a form of godliness but denying its power' (2 Tim. 3:5). And there have indeed been times in the history of the church when godlessness and a worldly spirit, with its preoccupation with forms and rituals, have been all too apparent. It was so when Jesus whipped the stall-holders and moneychangers out of the temple and exclaimed, 'Get these out of here! How dare you turn my Father's house into a market!' (John 2:16). He denounced the religious leaders for their hypocrisy: 'Now then, you Pharisees clean the outside of the cup and dish, but inside you are full of greed and wickedness' (Luke 11:39). He also criticized them for their ostentatious dress and love of formality: 'They like to walk around in flowing robes and be greeted in the market-places … and for a show make lengthy prayers' (Mark 12:38, 40).

When Paul speaks of 'a form of godliness', he means that it is possible to engage in the outward ritual of worship, in the hymns, the prayers and the liturgy, but know nothing of the inward power of the Holy Spirit. And without the reality of the presence and power of God, religion is an empty formality, and empty religion makes for empty souls of which we have more than enough in many churches today.

The church, a mixed company

Where these formalistic religionists are concerned, Paul's advice to Timothy is 'Have nothing to do with them'. He then explains why.

'They are the kind who worm their way into homes and gain control over weak-willed women, who are loaded down with sins and are swayed by all kinds of evil desires, always learning but never able to acknowledge the truth. Just as Jannes and Jambres opposed Moses, so also these men oppose the truth—men of depraved minds, who, as far as the faith is concerned, are rejected' (2 Tim. 3:6-8).

These people who emerge in the church in every age are very active in promoting falsehood and error under the guise of the church's message. At the time Paul was writing, these false teachers concentrated their efforts on influencing impressionable women, but in every age there are those who are easily influenced by the latest fashionable religious theory and by the love of novelty, as is clear from the number of sects and cults in existence today. But the distressing truth is that, even within the visible church itself, there are those in positions of leadership as ministers who are zealous in promoting a counterfeit faith. As Paul puts it: 'Just as Jannes and Jambres opposed Moses, so also these men oppose the truth—men of depraved minds, who, as far as the faith is concerned, are rejected' (2 Tim. 3:8).

> Satan was very active through the ministry of the false prophets, and it seemed, at times, as though God's purpose for his people would be totally crushed and defeated.

Jannes and Jambres are not mentioned in Scripture, but according to Jewish tradition they were the magicians who opposed Moses with their counterfeit and magic. Warning Timothy, Paul refers to them as an illustration of those who distort God's Word. We must bear in mind that the visible church will always be a mixed company of true and false confessors, as Jesus taught in his parable of the wheat and the tares (Matt. 13:24-30, 36-43). The field Jesus mentions is the world, but in part of it, which is God's kingdom where the wheat is sown, Satan has also sown tares. In the church on earth, there will always be those guilty of hypocrisy and external religiosity who will twist and distort the teaching of the Bible for their own ends.

But Paul assures Timothy that such falsehood cannot ultimately survive, and that God's truth will win out in the end. 'But they will not get very far because, as in the case of those men [Jannes and Jambres], their folly will be clear to everyone' (2 Tim. 3:9). But how can Paul be so sure of that? Because history testifies to it.

Throughout the Old Testament period, Satan was very active through the ministry of the false prophets, and it seemed, at times, as though God's purpose for his people would be totally crushed and defeated. But it did not happen. Similarly, in the New Testament period, and up to the present day, there have been 'terrible times' when it looked as though the church of God would be destroyed, and falsehood and error would triumph. But that has not happened, and it never will, for Christ has said, 'I will build my church, and the gates of Hades will not overcome it' (Matt. 16:18).

So we need not get depressed when we see the church going through a low period, as it is at the present time, for 'God's solid foundation stands firm, sealed with this inscription: "The Lord knows those who are his" ' (2 Tim. 2:19).

For further study ▶

FOR FURTHER STUDY

1. Study Ezekiel 13 and 33. How does this help you to understand the difference between the false and true prophet?

2. Read Isaiah 1 to see how God condemns the external forms of worship which are lacking in Spirit and power. What other examples of external worship are mentioned in the Bible?

3. To learn more about the 'last days', read Matthew 24 where Jesus talks about the end of Jerusalem, and the end of the Age. Go through the chapter carefully and see if you can trace the individual themes he mentioned.

TO THINK ABOUT AND DISCUSS

1. Do you think things are going to get easier for Christians in the country in which you live, or are they likely to become more difficult? Give a reason or reasons for your answer.

2. In the light of what Paul says about a 'form of godliness', there has to be a certain level of form and structure in church life and worship, for 'everything should be done in a fitting and orderly way' (1 Cor. 14:40). When can this cause a worship service potentially to become emptied of Spirit and power?

3. The sins Paul lists are still very much in existence today, but have people's attitudes towards them changed? If so, in what way or ways?

7 Continuing with Christ

(3:10-14)

This section begins with Paul contrasting two ways of life. In the previous passage, he described the spirit of godlessness that will characterize the lives of people in the last days, and which will even invade the church itself. There will be a steady decline in morals, and false teachers will arise who will distort the truth and who will only have 'a form of godliness, but deny its power'.

But Timothy, as a believer and a pastor, is to be different from that worldly spirit, even if it means he will have to suffer. As Paul puts it in verse 12, 'Everyone who wants to live a godly life in Christ Jesus will be persecuted'.

The Christian is different

There is a tendency in certain quarters of the church today to minimize the difference between life lived for Christ and the life lived in the world. The impression is given by some preachers that becoming a Christian need not entail any great change in life-style as long as one is prepared to give verbal assent to the Christian message. But Paul begins this section by saying to Timothy, 'You, however, know all about my teaching,' etc. He wants to emphasize the contrast between Timothy's ministry and the empty religion he has been describing in the previous paragraph.

> The Bible is quite explicit in teaching that the Christian has been called to a life of separation from the world—not in the sense of distancing ourselves from normal social interaction with people, but by resisting the pressures to conform to the world's values.

The Bible is quite explicit in teaching that the Christian has been called to a life of separation from the world—not in the sense of distancing ourselves from normal social interaction with people, but by resisting the pressures to conform to the world's values. Paul puts it plainly in his letter to the Roman Christians when he says, 'Do not conform any longer to the pattern of this world, but be transformed by the renewing of your mind' (Rom. 12:2). And there is no denying that the general 'pattern' of behaviour in our society is one of total and utter godlessness. A truly born-again Christian therefore will find that not only is there a 'renewing of [the] mind' that takes place, but also a renewing of his or her pattern of behaviour.

But we must also ask why this tendency exists in today's church to dilute, or play down, the difference between the Christian way and modern society's way. Is it that we do not want to offend members of the congregation by making little or no mention of such things as sin, holiness, hell and judgement? Is there some idea that we will turn people off Christianity by stressing these things as essential elements in the gospel? The truth is we shall never win worldly men or women for Christ by trying to like them, but only by showing how different they can be. After all, if there is no difference, surely there is no point in a person becoming a Christian in the first place!

Paul the role model

In the Christian life, as in other areas of human activity, it is always helpful and encouraging to have a role model to follow. If was like that with Paul and Timothy. The younger man had looked to the great apostle as a model for his own Christian life and ministry.

'You, however, know all about my teaching, my way of life, my purpose, faith, patience, love, endurance, persecutions, sufferings—what kinds of things happened to me in Antioch, Iconium and Lystra, the persecutions I endured. Yet the Lord rescued me from all of them. In fact, everyone who wants to live a godly life in Christ Jesus will be persecuted, while evil men and impostors will go from bad to worse, deceiving and being deceived. But as for you, continue in what you have learned and have become convinced of, because you know those from whom you learned it, and how from infancy you have known the holy Scriptures ...' (2 Tim. 3:10-15).

We must not think that Paul is being immodest or conceited in relating this list of virtues. Remember, he is in prison and is awaiting execution and he wants Timothy to understand how faithful God had been in undergirding his Christian life and preaching throughout his missionary journeys. Here are some of the things he mentions.

FIRST, he mentions his teaching of the Word of God. 'You, however, know all about my teaching...' The teaching and understanding of God's Word is fundamental to the life of the church and to the individual Christian. When difficulties arise, whether in the church or in our personal lives, it is from the teaching of Scripture that we receive wisdom for the task, and by its influence our own spirit is energized and refreshed. Paul will have a lot more to say about the teaching of Scripture in verses 16 and 17, but for the moment let us note that every church needs to be both a teaching and a learning church where the Bible is concerned.

Acts records that the members of the early church 'devoted themselves to the apostles' teaching' (Acts 2:42). They were not content with being saved from their sin, but they wanted to grow in their understanding of their new faith. A church may be humming like a dynamo with regard to its activities and organizations, but if its members are not receiving the solid exposition of God's Word, they are not going anywhere. Paul puts his teaching first because it underlies everything else he goes on to talk about, and it was the means by which Timothy was brought to Christ in the first place.

SECOND, Paul's teaching was amply confirmed by his godly life, and the consecrated purpose to serve God in his ministry even to the point of his present imprisonment—'my way of life, my purpose, faith, patience, love, endurance'. These qualities all followed from his profound conviction that the commands of God in the teaching of Scripture are meant to be obeyed, and the promises of God are true and reliable. Timothy had observed all this and sought to follow this model in his own life and ministry. And the same should be true of us. Our lifestyle and conduct should be determined by the values enshrined in the gospel, and not by the values of our secular society. Similarly, our purpose in life is to do God's will and to glorify Christ—both in our conduct and our service.

THIRD, when Paul goes on to talk about persecutions and sufferings, he was relating his own bitter experiences during his missionary journeys recorded in Acts. He mentions in particular three cities where he was treated badly— 'persecutions, sufferings—what kinds of things happened to me in Antioch, Iconium and Lystra, the persecutions I endured. Yet the Lord rescued me from all of them. In fact, everyone who wants to live a godly life in Christ Jesus will be persecuted, while evil men and impostors will go from bad to worse, deceiving and being deceived' (2 Tim. 3:11-13).

Timothy himself came from Lystra (Acts 16:1), and may have personally witnessed the occasion when Paul was stoned by a hostile mob and dragged out of the city and left for dead (Acts 14:19). In Antioch, the Jewish party incited the people to persecute Paul and Barnabas and had them driven out of the city (Acts 13:50). The same happened at Iconium where Paul and Barnabas narrowly escaped with their lives because of a conspiracy by Jews and Gentiles to stone them (Acts 14:5-6).

We may wonder how Paul and others like him could suffer such ill treatment and still continue in the work of the gospel. The only satisfactory explanation is that God gives a special grace and strength at such times. Paul himself simply says, 'Yet the Lord rescued me from all of them.' He also says that he was not unique in this, and that such persecution and suffering can be the lot of anyone who truly loves Christ. 'In fact, everyone who wants to live a godly life in Christ Jesus will be persecuted.'

Persecution for the sake of the gospel is inescapable, as Jesus made clear on several occasions. For example, 'Blessed are you when people insult you, persecute you and falsely say all kinds of evil against you because of me' (Matt. 5:11). Satan, the great adversary of our souls, never gives up in his attempts to destroy the faith of God's people, and always there are 'evil men', as Paul describes them, who are willing to be manipulated to do the devil's work. Today, persecution of the Christian faith is widespread in the world, in Nigeria, Pakistan, Indonesia and the Sudan to mention only a few countries. And even in western nations, evangelical Christians are coming under growing pressure, and in the future could be subjected to positive persecution. But our response must always be to remain firm in our convictions, to refuse to compromise, and to trust God absolutely for needed grace.

Continuing with Christ

Paul concludes this section by urging Timothy to continue with Christ in contrast with the 'evil men' mentioned in verse 13.

'But as for you, continue in what you have learned and have become convinced of ...' (2 Tim. 3:14a).

It is easy to begin a thing, but to continue with it is much more difficult. For instance, I could easily begin the Olympic marathon with all the other runners, but I doubt very much if I would be there at the finish. The physical stamina required is enormous, and without the long months of training beforehand, it becomes virtually impossible to cross the finishing line. The same is true at the spiritual level. We need spiritual stamina if we are to keep going in the Christian life. Jesus made that very point in several different ways.

'All men will hate you because of me, but he who stands firm to the end will be saved' (Matt. 10:22).

'If a man remains in me and I in him, he will bear much fruit' (John 15:5).

'No one who puts his hand to the plough and looks back is fit for service in the kingdom of God' (Luke 9:62).

Men or women who desire Christ, and set out on the way of discipleship, will find many escape routes looming up before them and many voices calling them to turn back. But if they are in earnest, they will not be distracted from their aim to follow Christ, or allow the seductions of the world to supersede his claim on their life.

Keep me from turning back.

The handles of my plough with tears are wet,

The shears with rust are spoiled, and yet, and yet

My God! My God! Keep me from turning back.[8]

For further study ▶

FOR FURTHER STUDY

1. To learn further of Paul's persecutions, study Acts 9:19-25, 13:42-52, 14:8-20, 16:16-40, 23:12-22.

2. Read through the gospels (or use a concordance or Bible computer software) and find out all that Jesus had to say about persecution, suffering and sacrifice for the kingdom of God.

TO THINK ABOUT AND DISCUSS

1. Paul urges Timothy to be different from people in the society in which he lived. Suggest several ways in which modern Christians may strive to be different from their unconverted neighbours, fellow students, family members and colleagues at work. What are the main areas of difficulty that believers face today in living distinctly different and separated lives?

2. Are we short of role models in today's church? What is your idea of the kind of role model the young Christian can follow? Can you think of a role model you followed as a young Christian? How might you become an effective mentor of others?

3. One quality of Christian character Paul mentions (2 Tim. 3:10) is patience. This is also an aspect of the fruit of the Spirit (Gal. 5:22). How are we to cultivate and demonstrate this?

8 The value of the Bible

(3:15-17)

The last chapter ended with Paul urging Timothy to continue with Christ, and with what he had learned from the teaching of God's Word. He gives two reasons why Timothy should be encouraged to do that.

First, 'because you know those from whom you learned it' (2 Tim. 3:14b). And who were they? His grandmother Lois and his mother Eunice who had instructed him in the Christian faith from his infancy (2 Tim. 1:5), and also Paul himself, whose teaching he had sought to follow.

Second, 'how from infancy you have known the holy Scriptures, which are able to make you wise for salvation through faith in Christ Jesus' (2 Tim. 3:15). Timothy had a sound knowledge of the Old Testament Scriptures, which he had received from his grandmother and his mother, and he believed those Scriptures to be the inspired Word of God. In the next couple of verses, Paul goes on to expand

> In spite of all attempts at times by emperors, dictators and totalitarian governments to destroy the Bible by burning, confiscation and the imprisonment and persecution of those who read it and preach it, all such attempts have miserably failed, and this remarkable book is still with us and is as widely dispersed as ever.

the inestimable value of the Scriptures.

'All Scripture is God-breathed and is useful for teaching, rebuking, correcting and training in righteousness, so that the man of God may be thoroughly equipped for every good work.'

The Bible's inspiration

'All Scripture is God-breathed.' That means the Bible owes its origin and its contents to the guidance and leading of the Holy Spirit. Peter puts it like this: 'No prophecy of Scripture came about by the prophet's own interpretation. For prophecy never had its origin in the will of man, but men spoke from God as they were carried along by the Holy Spirit' (2 Peter 1:20).

Nobody but the most prejudiced person would deny that the Bible is a unique book if only because, after existing for centuries, it continues to be taught, bought, distributed and loved more than any other book that has ever been written. But its true uniqueness lies in its unity, which is the hallmark of its divine inspiration. For the Bible is not just one book but a whole library of thirty-nine books in the Old Testament and twenty-seven in the New Testament. These were written over a period of some fifteen centuries by more than forty authors all of whom were different, including kings (David, Solomon), philosophers (Ecclesiastes), poets (Psalms), farmers (Amos), statesmen (Daniel), priests (Ezekiel, Ezra), prophets (Isaiah, Jeremiah), fishermen (Peter, John) and scholars like Paul. With such a variety of authorship over such a long period, one might expect the result to be a book that was no more than a mixed bag of ideas and inconsistencies. Instead, the Bible has a wonderful unity from Genesis to Revelation as it unfolds the single theme of God's plan of redemption.

Human inspiration, on the other hand, is something quite different. If we were to take some of the great writings of the world such as Plato, Aristotle, Josephus, Dante, Shakespeare etc., and join them in a single volume, all we would have would be a series of disconnected ideas and contradictions. There would be no unity or theme to hold the different books together as a single whole.

The inspiration of the Bible is also seen in its unique survival. All through history it has been a hated book for certain people because of its claim to be the word of the living God. But in spite of all attempts at times by emperors, dictators and totalitarian governments to destroy it by burning, confiscation and the imprisonment and persecution of those who read it and preach it, all such attempts have miserably failed—this remarkable book is still with us and is as widely dispersed as ever.

During the Stalin era in Russia, the Marxist government derided the Bible as a book full of legends, myths, and old wives' tales. It even established an anti-Bible museum in Moscow to try and convince the people. Yet for all their derision, the authorities were so desperately afraid that people would read it and believe it, that they put them in prison and in labour camps for doing so. Why? Because they knew that this unique book had the power to change people's lives.

Having stated that the Bible is the inspired Word of God, Paul now goes on to show its usefulness and purpose for the Christian—'and is useful for teaching, rebuking, correcting and training in righteousness'.

Teaching

We have already said quite a lot about the Bible's teaching. But Paul is now saying that Timothy should make good use of it as an indispensable instrument for teaching purposes. If I want to learn all about the history of our nation, I will read the history books, and if possible listen to those teachers who have access to the original sources and documents. Similarly, if I want to become more knowledgeable about the great doctrines of the Christian faith, I will set myself the task of studying the original sources in the Bible, for it imparts the knowledge of God's ultimate revelation in Jesus Christ.

When people are in earnest in their pursuit of the truth of God's Word, they are not dependent on their own intellectual capacity alone, but are helped by the indwelling Holy Spirit. Christ said, 'When he, the Spirit of truth, comes, he will guide you into all truth' (John 16:13). Therefore, when we read and study the Bible's teaching, the Holy Spirit enlightens our minds and understanding, and directs its truth to our hearts. In this way, we are able to discern between truth and falsehood, and will not fall for everything we hear or read because it comes from a bishop, theologian or pastor.

Rebuking

The Bible not only teaches the truth of God, but it also teaches the truth about ourselves, and gives many warnings and rebukes about our conduct and discipleship. It is a very honest book, and it never whitewashes any of God's servants who appear in its pages. Their faults and failings are all clearly set forth so that we may learn from them.

> When people are in earnest in their pursuit of the truth of God's Word, they are not dependent on their own intellectual capacity alone, but are helped by the indwelling Holy Spirit.

As for ourselves, when we read the Bible we are made to take the blinkers off and see ourselves as we really are in the sight of God—and that can be a painful experience. We constantly fall into sin and give way to temptation, and when we come to the Word of God it rebukes us. We may succeed in keeping our conscience quiet for a time, as long as we keep clear of the Bible. But the moment we start reading it, there will be verses and passages that make us feel extremely uncomfortable because they bring home to us that we have grieved God's Spirit. And until we take the rebuke to heart—in repentance and confession—we will never know inner peace, or make further progress in our discipleship.

In his capacity as a pastor and Christian leader, Timothy is to make good use of the Bible as a teaching tool to rebuke others when they fall into doctrinal error concerning doctrine, or, by their conduct, bring the church of God into disrepute. Later, when giving a charge to Timothy to preach the gospel, Paul tells him plainly that he is to rebuke his people when they fall into sin (2 Tim. 4:2). But whenever the Bible has to be used in this way, that is, to warn and reprove a fellow Christian, it should be done in a spirit of love.

Correcting and training in righteousness

It is not enough that we should be rebuked by the Word of God when we go astray and fall into sin; we also need to be corrected as to how we should live in order to please God. And this, too, the Bible is able to do. It corrects our wrong thinking, and trains or instructs us in the way of righteousness, the right path we are to follow if we want to grow in godliness and holiness of life. As the psalmist says, 'Your word is a lamp to my feet and a light for my path' (Ps. 119:105).

This illumination upon our path through life comes from the many directives we have in the Scriptures concerning different aspects of life—our use of time, family life, the use of money, the rearing of children, marriage, sexual relations, etc. In all these things, broad principles and guidelines are laid down which help to train us in the life of righteousness. It is like listening to a form of preaching. To quote J I Packer, 'Holy Scripture should be thought of as God preaching— God preaching to me every time I read or hear any part of it—God the Father preaching God the Son in the power of God the Holy Spirit'.[9]

Equipped for work

Paul concludes this section by stating the purpose underlying our desire to read and study the Scriptures. '…So that the man of God may be thoroughly equipped for every good work' (2 Tim. 3:17). The expression 'man of God' would refer in the first instance to Timothy and other pastors, who need to be equipped with the authority of Scripture to teach and lead God's people. But it can equally apply to all Christians. For we all need to reach maturity in Christ, and it is only by our diligent study of the Bible that we can become thoroughly equipped in knowledge, faith and holiness to do God's work.

For further study ▶

FOR FURTHER STUDY

1. For the use of the Scriptures in preaching and teaching, see Peter's sermon, Acts 2:14-41; Stephen's address, Acts 7:1-53; and Paul's preaching, Acts 13:13-52.

2. Read Jeremiah 36 as an example of the way God inspired his servants to write the Scriptures.

TO THINK ABOUT AND DISCUSS

1. Timothy owed much to his Christian grandmother and mother. Do you think Christian parents and grandparents today are placing sufficient importance on giving their children instruction in the gospel from an early age? What hinders them from doing so? How could some of these obstacles be overcome?

2. Discuss the differences between divine inspiration and human inspiration.

3. The Bible teaches us the truth about God, the truth about ourselves, and the truth about the world in which we live. Do you agree with these statements, and if so in what way would you claim them to be true?

4. In what way does a prayerful and regular reading and study of the Bible help a person to develop a consistent world view? Suggest how this affects one's view of

(a) the sanctity of life for the unborn, terminally ill, and elderly people;

(b) marriage and the family;

(c) the work ethic.

9 A solemn charge

(4:1-8)

In this fourth chapter we have possibly the last words of Paul to the church. He is shortly to be executed, as he reminds us in verse 6: 'For I am already being poured out like a drink offering, and the time has come for my departure.' For thirty years or more, he had laboured in the work of the gospel, and now his life is to be poured out as a final offering to his Saviour, the Lord Jesus Christ.

Accordingly, he is terribly anxious that Timothy should be faithful in preaching the gospel, and with great solemnity he charges him to do this as in the very presence of God.

'In the presence of God and of Christ Jesus, who will judge the living and the dead, and in view of his appearing and his kingdom, I give you this charge' (2 Tim. 4:1).

A divine mandate

Bearing in mind that this was a time when evil men and impostors were seeking to destroy the faith, and that Timothy was a man of timid disposition, he must have trembled when he read this charge, especially since it came as a command from God. Nor should we overlook the fact that it is a charge applicable to all pastors, and for that matter, to all Christians.

Timothy and all ministers are to carry out their ministry under the very eye of God. Moreover, when Christ returns to this earth to establish his eternal kingdom, and to judge the living and the dead, pastors and all other servants of God will have to give an account. Such a thought must surely act as a great incentive to all pastors to take their calling very seriously. They must not be so concerned to please their congregations, or be influenced by the criticism or praise of others to the extent that they forget that they are accountable to God in Christ.

James, in his letter, takes this whole question of pastoral accountability a step further, and warns that those who are teachers of God's truth will be under greater condemnation than others if they are not faithful in preaching that truth. 'Not many of you should presume to be teachers, my brothers, because you know that we who teach will be judged more strictly' (James 3:1). He emphasizes the privilege of the preaching ministry, but—like Paul—he also cautions the preacher to remember that responsibility carries accountability with it.

Next Paul goes on to give the content of the charge.

'Preach the Word; be prepared in season and out of season; correct, rebuke and encourage—with great patience and careful instruction' (2 Tim. 4:2).

Preach the word

The first thing Timothy must do is give priority to the act of preaching. The word translated 'preaching' actually means to 'herald' or 'proclaim'. This is the pastor's most important function, and must not be displaced by his other duties. Thomas Watson, the Puritan, once said, 'God had only one Son, and he made him a preacher'—and this is perfectly true. If we study the ministry of Jesus in the Gospels, we shall find that, although he performed many miracles, and showed great compassion in healing people's bodies, the greater part of his ministry was given to preaching. Mark begins his Gospel with the words: 'After John was put in prison, Jesus went into Galilee, proclaiming the good news of God' (Mark 1:14). And at the end of his ministry Jesus commissioned his followers to 'Go into all the word and preach the good news' (Mark 16:15).

But equally important as the need to have preaching in today's church is the question: What are we to preach? What should preachers be communicating to the people in their congregations? Paul's answer in his charge to Timothy is clear—he is to 'preach the Word'. Preaching is not merely a speech or address on a religious topic. Neither is it man's word about God. Rather, it is God's word to man. The preacher is not in the pulpit to ventilate his own ideas and opinions on the human condition and world affairs, but to expound the Scriptures. J I Packer spells out the function of the preacher with great clarity in the following passage:

> … The evangelical preacher will relate the specific content of all his messages to Christ, His mediation, His cross and resurrection, and His gift of new life to those who trust Him. In that sense the preacher will imitate Paul, who when he visited Corinth "resolved to know nothing, except Jesus Christ and him crucified" (1 Cor. 2:2). That does not mean, of course, that the evangelical preacher will harp all the time on the bare fact of the crucifixion. It means rather that he will use all lines of biblical thought to illuminate the meaning of that fact; and he will never let his exposition get detached from Calvary's cross and the redemption that was wrought there. In this way he will sustain a Christ-centred, cross-oriented preaching ministry with an evangelistic as well as a pastoral thrust.[10]

The urgency in preaching

'Be prepared in season and out of season' (2 Tim. 4:2). This command contains several aspects of meaning—'be ready', 'have a sense of urgency, 'be insistent', be earnest'.

Richard Baxter, the Puritan preacher, once said, 'I preached as never sure to preach again; as a dying man to dying men.' That is urgency! He meant that in the light of eternity, time is short, and the message of God's salvation is a matter of life and death which people must hear. He was echoing the words of Jesus: 'As long as it is day, we must do the work of him who sent me. Night is coming, when no one can work' (John 9:4).

This urgent preaching must take every opportunity to declare the gospel: 'In season or out of season', 'convenient or inconvenient' (NEB). There are times when preaching is a great joy and one feels carried along by a mysterious power. But there are also times when it is uphill work, either because one does not feel up to it, or the congregation appears unresponsive. But the preacher must not become the victim of moods. Consecrated persistence is the order of the day, and that will keep him going 'in season and out of season'.

> Richard Baxter, the puritan preacher, once said, 'I preached as never sure to preach again; as a dying man to dying men.'

Urgent preaching is also preaching with conviction and earnestness. Preaching is a serious business and the preacher should never give people the impression that what he is dealing with is something of no great importance. If he himself is not moved and captivated by the gospel message, there is little chance that the congregation will be. To quote Richard Baxter again:

> Let the people see that you are in good earnest. ...You cannot break men's hearts by jesting with them, or telling them a smooth tale, or patching up a gaudy oration. Men will not cast away their dearest pleasures upon a drowsy request of one that seemeth not to mean as he speaks, or to care much whether his request be granted. [11]

When dealing with themes such as the grace of God to sinners, the judgement to come, and the death and resurrection of Christ, the preacher surely cannot be anything other than in deadly earnest.

Applying the Word

Paul goes on to suggest different ways in which the preacher is to apply the Word of God in different situations—'correct, rebuke, and encourage'.

Correction is required because people in the congregation can sometimes have very confused ideas about the gospel, and by sound reasoning from the Scriptures the preacher can set them right in their thinking.

When Paul says the preacher is to 'rebuke' in the course of preaching, he does not mean he will cultivate a condemnatory style in which he preaches 'at' people rather than 'to' people. The writer to the Hebrews describes the Word of God as 'living and active. Sharper than any double-edged sword, it penetrates even to dividing soul and spirit, joints and marrow; it judges the thoughts and attitudes of the heart' (Heb. 4:12).

Biblical preaching will therefore do its own rebuking and judging, convicting people of sin and bringing them to repentance.

But people are not only to be rebuked because of their failings—they must also be encouraged, is the point Paul makes. In the congregation there will be those who are depressed, those who have all kinds of fears and foreboding, those facing difficult situations, and so on. All these, as they listen to the Word of God, will need a certain 'lift' to their spirits to remind them of God's keeping grace, and to help them restore their vision of the triumph of the gospel.

The preacher has to do all these things! No wonder Paul himself said on one occasion, 'And who is equal to such a task?' But then adds, '...but our competence comes from God' (2 Cor. 2:16, 3:5).

The preacher's manner

How is this great and difficult task of preaching to be done? Paul answers, '...with great patience and careful instruction' (2 Tim. 4:2). There *are* no short cuts to a spiritually successful ministry. It calls for patience and perseverance, and a refusal to use pressure techniques to make people 'decide' for Christ. The preacher's responsibility is to declare faithfully the gospel message, and the results must be left to the work of the Holy Spirit. He is the One who will convict of sin and bring people to repentance, and he will use faithful preaching to do that.

God's servant will also exercise great patience at the pastoral level, if he is not to become disillusioned in the early years of ministry. He must be realistic in his dealings with people, for they can backslide, grow cold in their love for God, let one down again and again, and prove utterly faithless. But the pastor will not give up on them; he will bear with them patiently while trying to change them through 'careful instruction'. It will help in this direction if he keeps reminding himself of how patient God is with us in our failures.

Rejection of the truth

In the next couple of verses, Paul goes on to give Timothy the reason why 'careful instruction' in the Word of God is so important and necessary.

'For the time will come when men will not put up with

sound doctrine. Instead, to suit their own desires, they will gather around them a great number of teachers to say what their itching ears want to hear. They will turn their ears away from the truth and turn aside to myths'(2 Tim. 4:3-4).

Commenting on these verses, William Hendriksen says, 'In every period of history there will be a season during which men refuse to listen to sound doctrine. As history continues onward toward the consummation, this situation grows worse, men will not endure to tolerate the truth.'[12]

We are certainly passing through one of those periods today in the church in the west. There are many 'itching ears', even within evangelical churches. The itch for 'novelty', or 'something more' than the sound teaching of the Word of God, has led many to focus on feelings and experience. But feelings are changeable, and can never be a firm enough foundation for building up one's spiritual life.

Standing firm

Paul finally sums it all up saying to Timothy, 'But you, keep your head in all situations, endure hardship, do the work of an evangelist, discharge all the duties of your ministry' (2 Tim. 4:5).

Whatever the prevailing theological fashions of his day, Timothy, as God's servant, is not to be influenced by them. He will not take his lead from what others are doing. Let them get on with their 'itching' novelties, and their readiness to satisfy the unhealthy craving for the sensational. Timothy must remain clear-headed and stand firm on the great doctrines of the cross, the empty tomb, and the return of the Lord Jesus Christ in glory and power. Nor should he forget that he is an evangelist and must therefore have a real burden for the souls of men and women, and seek to win them for Christ.

The same sound advice applies to the evangelical minister of today. He must not forever be looking over his shoulder at other churches, and their slick 'short-cut' methods of building up their congregations. There are no short cuts to building up a church. Ministry is hard, painstaking work, and God requires his servants, in the first instance, not to be 'successful', but to be faithful. The success or otherwise can be safely left in his hands.

Continuity of God's work

It is important to notice the word 'for' with which the final section of this paragraph begins. 'For I am already being poured out like a drink offering, and the time has come for my departure' (2 Tim. 4:6). The link is clearly seen with what Paul had said earlier. It is as if he is saying, 'Timothy, be faithful, because I won't be in this world

> Whatever the prevailing theological fashions of his day, Timothy is not to be influenced by them. Let others get on with their 'itching' novelties, and their readiness to satisfy the unhealthy craving for the sensational. Timothy must remain clear-headed and stand firm on the great doctrines of the cross, the empty tomb, and the return of the Lord Jesus Christ in glory and power.

much longer, my end is near and my life will shortly be poured out on the altar of sacrifice—but you must carry on God's work.'

We learn from this that the work of God is always greater than the instrument that he uses. No one is indispensable in God's cause. Eli dies, but God raises up Samuel; Joshua follows Moses; and when Elijah is taken up to heaven, a double portion of his prophetic spirit falls on Elisha. So now Paul faces martyrdom, but Timothy is to follow on. John Wesley once said, 'God buries his workmen, but carries on his work.' In his mercy and grace, God may use us in his work, but he never has to depend on us. The gospel is far bigger. That is a humbling thought, but it helps us to keep our place in God's scheme of things in true perspective.

When Paul speaks of his 'departure', the underlying idea is of a ship slipping its moorings and setting out to sea. He is about to 'weigh anchor' and set out on the final voyage to his heavenly home. We shall all 'weigh anchor' one day; in the meantime, if God has given us work to do, let us do it as faithfully and conscientiously as we can.

The fight, race, and crown

There now follow three images in which Paul looks back over some thirty years of faithful and diligent ministry. (2 Tim. 4:7-8).

'I have fought the good fight.' In speaking of 'the fight', Paul has in mind the wrestling or boxing matches in the sporting arena. When the contestant has put every ounce of energy into the match and given of his best, he will experience a deep sense of satisfaction. The apostle feels the same way about the fight he was engaged in with the principalities and powers of darkness.

As Christians we are all engaged in the same fight with sin and temptation in our own hearts, as well as against the forces of evil operating in society. The question is: are we winning? Do we have a sense of satisfaction that we have given of our best in the warfare, and can say, at this moment, 'I have fought a good fight'?

'I have finished the race'. This was not literally true for Paul in the sense that his life was ended, for his martyrdom had not yet occurred. But it *was* true in the sense that he had finished the course of his ministry in spite of the obstacles of persecution, hardship, criticism, and desertion by friends. Through it all he had never allowed himself to be diverted from the course, but had kept straight on looking only to Jesus, the goal and objective of his faith.

Hebrews 12:1-2 reminds us that the Christian race both begins with Christ, and ends with Christ. Furthermore, we should think of it more as a marathon than a sprint. The sprint requires a short, staccato burst of energy—and some Christians are like that. They are full of enthusiasm for a short time but then it dies. The marathon, on the other hand, calls for staying power, and the

> As Christians we are all engaged in the same fight with sin and temptation in our own hearts, as well as against the forces of evil operating in society. The question is: are we winning?

determination to keep going in spite of the world, the flesh, and the devil.

'I have kept the faith. Now there is in store for me the crown of righteousness, which the Lord, the righteous Judge, will award to me on that day—and not only to me, but also to all who have longed for his appearing' (2 Tim. 4:8).

Still with the sporting imagery, the underlying idea is the laurel wreath with which the victor was crowned. But whereas this wreath would quickly fade and die, Paul has in mind the crown of everlasting life, which is the prize he will receive from Christ for his faithfulness in preaching the gospel.

And then for our encouragement he quickly adds that it is the reward all believers will receive when this life is done, if they have fought the fight, run the race, and kept the faith.

FOR FURTHER STUDY

1. Trace the ministry of Jesus in the Gospels and identify the occasions where preaching and teaching were given priority over healing, miracles, etc.

2. When Philip preached Christ to the Ethiopian (Acts 8) he only had the Old Testament. In the light of Luke 24, look for other passages in the Old Testament that can be used to preach Christ.

TO THINK ABOUT AND DISCUSS

1. How is the Christian minister to balance his accountability to his members for his ministry with his accountability to God?

2. Timothy was to give priority to preaching and teaching in his ministry. Is the same priority evident in the ministry in your church or fellowship? If not, why not? What could you do, as an ordinary church member or church officer, to encourage and facilitate the place of expository Bible preaching and teaching each Sunday and through the week during fellowship meetings?

3. Is there a place for humour in preaching?

4. How would you distinguish between the preaching and teaching aspects of the Christian ministry? Do some ministers show a stronger ability in one or other of these aspects?

10 Final words and greetings

(4:9-22)

After his solemn charge to Timothy, and his confident assertion that the 'crown of righteousness' awaited him in the future, Paul's thoughts in this final paragraph are centred on his present situation in the Roman dungeon. What follows is a truly human cry, in which the apostle expresses his personal needs, makes certain requests, and sends his final greeting.

His loneliness

'Do your best to come to me quickly, for Demas, because he loved this world, has deserted me and has gone to Thessalonica. Crescens has gone to Galatia, and Titus to Dalmatia. Only Luke is with me. Get Mark and bring him with you because he is helpful to me in my ministry. I sent Tychicus to Ephesus' (2 Tim. 4:9-12).

Clearly, Paul was suffering from a deep sense of isolation

and loneliness in his damp prison cell, and he longs for the companionship of Timothy in these last days of his life. There is a note of urgency in his request for Timothy to 'come to me quickly', which is repeated in verse 21: 'Do your best to get here before winter.' In the ancient world, sailing and navigation could be impossible once the winter weather had set in (see Acts 27), and Paul's need for Timothy to ease his loneliness was urgent. He was shortly to be executed.

We sometimes make the mistake of regarding the characters in the Bible as super-people, rather than as ordinary folk like ourselves. From a passage like this, and there are many others, we can see that even a spiritual giant like Paul was a frail human being with needs like our own. James makes this point when speaking of Elijah. 'Elijah was a man just like us. He prayed earnestly that it would not rain, and it did not rain on the land for three and a half years. Again he prayed, and the heavens gave rain, and the earth produced its crops' (James 5:17-18). Elijah's prayer was heard because he trusted God absolutely, and not because he was a super-man.

One reason Paul gives for his loneliness is that his friends had left him. Demas had actually 'deserted' him in his time of need, and the others, Crescens, Titus, and Tychicus had left to carry out the Lord's work elsewhere. It reminds us of the loneliness Jesus must have felt when his disciples deserted him at his arrest in the garden of Gethsemane. 'Then everyone deserted him and fled' (Mark 14:50).

Loneliness is a dreadful experience, and not something God intended for people. On the contrary, we were made for friendship and togetherness. At the dawn of creation, God said, 'It is not good for the man to be alone. I will make a helper suitable for him' (Gen. 2:18). And the psalmist says, 'God sets the lonely in families' (Ps. 68:6). We all need to have a sense of belonging, to a family, a community, a circle of friends, etc. That is why our fellowship together is so important in the life of the church, the household and family of God. When people come into our church they should find it to be warm and welcoming, else its purpose is defeated.

There is more than one kind of loneliness. It does not have to be physical—it can be spiritual or emotional. The Christian worker can experience a sense of failure and loneliness when there is little response to his or her efforts. Elijah felt like that and actually prayed that he might die, for he felt he was the only one left, and no one else cared about God's cause (1 Kings 19). But when we are tempted to feel that way, we must remind ourselves that we are not really alone, for God himself has given us his promise, 'Never will I leave you; never will I forsake you' (Heb. 13:5).

His sense of hurt

Paul's humanness can also be seen in his deep sense of hurt at the conduct of Demas, who was once a close friend and fellow-worker. 'Demas, because he loved this world, has deserted me and has gone to Thessalonica.' Desertion is a form of betrayal; it is turning one's back upon someone in the time of crisis when that person needs our help and support. But what hurt Paul most of all was the reason Demas deserted him— 'because he loved this world'. He was, in fact, a backslider because he not only deserted Paul, but the Lord Jesus and his gospel. There was a time when Demas was faithful to the Lord and is mentioned in two other places. 'Our dear friend Luke, the doctor, and Demas send greetings' (Col. 4:14). 'Demas and Luke, my fellow-workers' (Philem. 24).

The Christian is a citizen of two worlds. Millions know and love only this world—with its loves and joys, its hates and pleasures. And while the Christian also lives in this world, and loves its joys and pleasures, he also knows and loves even more that other eternal world to which Christ is drawing him ever closer with each day. Demas had forgotten that, and had allowed the glamour of this world to seduce him from his love for Christ.

It can happen to any one of us. We can so easily become infected by the pagan world around us, with its false values and godless spirit. To prevent it happening, we must be continually on our guard, allowing the Holy Spirit to direct and control our lives from within. J B Phillips translates Romans 12:2 as follows: 'Don't let the world around you squeeze you into its own mould, but let God remould your minds from within.'

> The Christian is a citizen of two worlds. Millions know and love only this world—with its loves and joys, its hates and pleasures. And while the Christian also lives in this world, and loves its joys and pleasures, he also knows and loves even more that other eternal world to which Christ is drawing him ever closer with each day.

Demas was not the only one to desert Paul in the time of need. 'At my first defence, no one came to my support, but everyone deserted me. May it not be held against them' (2 Tim. 4:16). This again must have been particularly hurtful since at his preliminary trial there was not a single person from the Christian community in Rome to speak in his defence. He was all alone. In the Christian life there will be occasions, mercifully rare, when we have to stand alone, when every prop is taken away, and we have nothing left to lean on but the grace and integrity of our God.

That was how Paul saw it. 'But the Lord stood at my side and gave me strength, so that through me the message might be fully proclaimed and all the Gentiles might hear it. And I was delivered from the lion's mouth. The Lord will rescue me from every evil attack and will bring me safely to his heavenly kingdom. To him be glory for ever and ever. Amen.' (2 Tim. 4:18).

His physical and intellectual needs

'When you come, bring the cloak that I left with Carpus at Troas, and my scrolls, especially the parchments' (2 Tim. 4:13).

We have already seen that winter was coming on, and in his cold, miserable cell, Paul was beginning to feel the cold, hence his request for the cloak he had left with Carpus. This was a heavy woollen blanket with a V-shaped opening for the head, and slits at the side for the arms to go through, and the request itself is again one of those human touches that shows the great apostle to be a frail human being with ordinary needs. Commentators frequently point to the similarity with the plight of that other great instrument of God's truth, William Tyndale, in his letter written from his cell at Vilvorde, and which is equally touching.

> Wherefore I beg your lordship, and that by the Lord Jesus, that if I am to remain here through the winter, you will request the commissary to have the kindness to send me, from the goods of mine which he has, a warmer cap; for I suffer greatly from cold in the head ... a warmer coat also, for this which I have is very thin; a piece of cloth too to patch my leggings. My overcoat is worn out; my shirts are also worn out. He has a woollen shirt, if he will be good enough to send it. But most of all I beg and beseech your clemency to be urgent with the commissary, that he will kindly permit me to have the Hebrew Bible, Hebrew grammar, and Hebrew dictionary, that I may pass the time in that study.[13]

Paul also requested Timothy to bring 'my scrolls, especially the parchments'. He not only needed warm clothes for his body, but books to keep his mind active. The scrolls may have been writing materials, whereas the parchments would have been books, possibly copies of the Old Testament. The important thing in all we have said about Paul's needs is that we should never despise the gifts and blessings of God's common grace to humanity. As John Stott wisely says:

> When our spirit is lonely we need friends. When our body is cold we need clothing. When our mind is bored we need books. To admit this is not unspiritual; it is human. These are the natural needs of mortal men and women.[14]

Final greetings

Greet Priscilla and Aquila and the household of Onesiphorus. Erastus stayed in Corinth, and I left Trophimus sick in Miletus. Do your best to get here before winter. Eubulus greets you, and so do Pudens, Linus, Claudia and all the brothers. The Lord be with your spirit. Grace be with you' (2 Tim. 4:19-22).

In the introduction to the beginning of this book, a brief mention was made of the different personalities mentioned in 2 Timothy, several of whom appear in this list of greetings. Some of them are simply names to us, but, when reading the book of Acts, we get glimpses into the lives of one or two others. For example Priscilla and Aquila are mentioned several times in Acts. They were a godly couple and were great friends of Paul.

But a passage like this is not without meaning. For instance, we learn from it that, in his sovereign purpose, God chooses often to work in the church through ordinary faithful believers, like some of those mentioned above. Undoubtedly, God does have special people for special tasks, like Paul and Timothy, but the ongoing work of witness and prayer is carried on by countless thousands of ordinary Christians whose names will never appear in the annals of history.

We thank God therefore for these people who are the backbone of the local church, and we pray for them the prayer with which Paul ends this letter. 'The Lord be with your spirit. Grace be with you.'

FOR FURTHER STUDY

1. With the help of a concordance or Bible software, work through Acts and the letters of Paul and find out all you can about that remarkable couple, Aquila and Priscilla.

2. Apart from Paul and Timothy, look for other characters in the Bible who were chosen by God as special men or women for special tasks, and study their lives to see what you can learn.

TO THINK ABOUT AND DISCUSS

1. Do you agree that we sometimes make the mistake of thinking of Bible characters as super-spiritual when in fact they were, really, ordinary people whom God chose to use?

2. Towards the end of his life, Paul experienced profound loneliness. What ideas can you come up with to alleviate the loneliness of vulnerable people in your church?

3. Consider the example of Demas in Scripture. Is there any way in which we can distinguish between the person who is a true backslider, and the person who was not truly a Christian in the first instance? Does the teaching of Christ in the parable of the sower (Luke 8:1-15) help to clarify this matter?

4. Paul needed his books, even in prison, to stimulate his mind and feed his soul and spirit. Are Christians reading in your church? Are you a reader? How can you help people to become avid readers of Christian books?

Endnotes

1 William Hendriksen, *2 Timothy*, Banner of Truth, p.49

2 John Stott, *Guard the Gospel*, IVP p.54

3 J C Ryle, *Holiness*, Evangelical Press p21

4 *2 Timothy*, Banner of Truth p.260

5 Leslie F Church, *Knight of the Burning Heart*, Wyvern Books, p.122

6 Quoted in *The Times*, 24 January 2004

7 Word Publishing U.K. Ltd, p.11

8 Quoted by William MacDonald in *True Discipleship*

9 *God has Spoken*, Hodder and Stoughton, 1975

10 Ed. Samuel T. Logan Introduction to *Preaching,* Evangelical Press

11 *The Reformed Pastor*, Epworth Press, 1950, p.145

12 *1 and 2 Timothy and Titus*, Banner of Truth, 1960

13 Quoted by Brian Edwards *God's outlaw,* Evangelical Press, p164

14 John Stott, *2 Timothy*, p.121

The Opening up series

Opening up Exodus	Opening up Ezra
Opening up Psalms	Opening up Ecclesiastes
Opening up Ezekiel's visions	Opening up Amos
Opening up Nahum	Opening up 1 Corinthians

Further titles in preparation

Opening up Philippians

Opening up Colossians and Philemon

Opening up 1 Thessalonians

Opening up 1 Timothy

This fine series is aimed at the 'average person in the church' and combines brevity, accuracy and readability with an attractive page layout. Thought-provoking questions make the books ideal for both personal or small group use.

'Laden with insightful quotes and penetrating practical application, Opening up Philippians is a Bible study tool which belongs on every Christian's bookshelf!'

DR. PHIL ROBERTS, PRESIDENT, MIDWESTERN BAPTIST THEOLOGICAL SEMINARY, KANSAS CITY, M I S S O U R I

Please contact us for a free catalogue

In the UK ☎ 01568 613 740   **email—** sales@dayone.co.uk

In the United States: ☎ Toll Free:1-8-morebooks

In Canada: ☎ 519 763 0339 www.dayone.co.uk